HISTORY OF NEW TESTAMENT TIMES IN PALESTINE
175 B.C.-70 A.D.

SHAILER MATHEWS, A.M.
PROFESSOR OF NEW TESTAMENT HISTORY AND
INTERPRETATION IN THE UNIVERSITY OF CHICAGO

First published by The MacMillan Company in 1908.

Copyright © Shailer Mathews.

This edition published in 2018.

TABLE OF CONTENTS

CHAPTER I: THE JEWS UNDER THE SELEUCIDAE

THE conquests of Alexander began a new era for Palestine as well as for other regions of the East. After his victory over Darius III at Issus (333), Alexander advanced steadily, conquering Damascus and the cities along the Mediterranean coast, finally coming to Tyre, which refused to surrender. Thereupon began the famous siege, which, after seven months, resulted in the complete overthrow of the city, two thousand of its inhabitants being hanged upon its walls, and thirty thousand being sold into slavery. Just as he was entering upon this siege, Alexander summoned the Jews to renounce their allegiance to Persia, furnish him with provisions, and pay him such tribute as they had been accustomed to pay Darius III. Jaddua, the high priest, refused to obey, pleading his oath of allegiance to Darius. Alexander consequently threatened him with severe punishment, and after he had reduced Tyre, had allowed the Samaritans to establish a rival religion upon Mount Gerizim, and had taken Gaza, he proceeded against Jerusalem. Josephus's account of the events that followed, although not beyond question, is possibly correct in its main features. On the arrival of Alexander at Scopus, he was met by Jaddua and a train of priests in their robes and a great multitude in white garments. The sight awoke the religious reverence of the young conqueror, and he treated the city with favour, even offering a sacrifice in the temple. He further granted the Jews the privilege of living in accordance with their own laws, and freed them from tribute during the sabbatical year. Palestine, however, was incorporated in the satrapy of Coele-Syria, with Samaria as its capital. The subsequent revolt of the Samaritans brought punishment only on themselves, and Judea was left in peace throughout Alexander's life, Jewish customs and prejudices being treated with consideration.

With the later career of Alexander Jewish history has little direct concern, but his policy of binding together his vast empire by a Greek civilisation was to be of almost fatal influence upon the nation. The realisation of this magnificent conception was prevented by Alexander's early death (June 13, 323 B.C.), but its fundamental idea, the unification of an empire by a common religion and civilisation, was inherited by his successors. If Alexander indeed failed to establish a lasting empire, his efforts resulted in the Graeco-Oriental civilisation.

In the division of the Macedonian Empire among the Diadochi, or successors of Alexander, Coele-Syria fell to Laomedon. Ptolemy Lagus, who had received Egypt, proceeded at once to conquer Palestine and entered Jerusalem one Sabbath, on the plea of wishing to sacrifice. As a result of his suzerainty many Jews were carried or emigrated to Alexandria and other cities of Egypt and Africa, Judea remaining in possession of the Ptolemies during the third century, though not without brief intervals of subjection to Syria. During these years the condition of Judea was not unprosperous, as little was demanded of the high priest except the annual tribute of twenty talents of silver.

In government Judea was a somewhat remarkable combination of a city-state and a theocracy. The high priest had political as well as religious supremacy, but associated with him was the Gerousia, or Senate of Jerusalem. Whether or not this body was the outgrowth of some ancient municipal institution of the Hebrews, or resulted from the influence of Hellenistic life cannot be determined with certainty. Possibly it was the outgrowth of the assembly of the heads of the 150 leading families which appears in the days of Nehemiah, but beyond the fact that it was aristocratic and composed of priests and elders we know little. The Jewish people could meet, perhaps, in popular bodies, but about this there is again little information. In a word, Judea was Jerusalem and its "daughters."

The extent of this city-state during the Egyptian and Syrian suzerainty, while not definitely known, was certainly inconsiderable. Neither Samaria nor Galilee was included, nor the country east of Jordan, nor any considerable part of the maritime plain

Nor are the relations of Judea, with Egypt and Syria, altogether clear. Each was in turn its suzerain, and, in fact, at one time it would seem as if, perhaps because of intermarriage, the Jewish tribute was divided between the two suzerains. But such an arrangement was but short-lived, and whether Egypt or Syria was for the time being dominant, the Jews were locally subject to this high priest, who saw to it that the tribute of 20 talents was farmed out, collected, and, with the Temple tax of 10,000 drachmas, paid. It is not clear that there was always a representative of the sovereign in Jerusalem, although the Seleucid house was later represented in the person of the eparch a sort of early burg-graf.

Of even more significance than these outward political relations was the threefold development which, during the years of political change following the death of Alexander the Great, characterised the inner life of the Jews that of "wisdom" literature, of the ritual and priesthood and of legalism. In all of these particulars Jewish history is unique, but perhaps in none more unique than in the collection of proverbs and practical advice to be found in such writings as our canonical Proverbs, Job, and Ecclesiastes, and such other writings as the Wisdom of Jesus the Son of Sirach, and the Wisdom of Solomon. Like the other two tendencies, this is rooted deep in the history of the Hebrew race, for wise sayings of very ancient origin are to be found in its early literature. But during the post-exilic period, and especially after the Greek influence began to be felt, "wisdom" found its most remarkable expression and became a literary form. To speak of its literature in detail is impossible, but one cannot overlook its knowledge of the world and its cynicism, as well as its more common characteristics, sobriety, and moral earnestness.

But good advice is seldom more than a luxury, and the history of the Jews was to centre about the struggles between the two other tendencies which began during these years to show themselves so clearly. Indeed, the two hundred and fifty or three hundred years preceding the destruction of Jerusalem by Titus may be said to be filled with little else than the gradual and unobserved triumph of legalism in the persons of the Pharisees over ritualism, whether in the persons of the Sadducees or of the nation as a whole.

At the outset the two forces were in harmony. The Jewish state was a theocracy, the high priest at its head being held responsible for the tribute until Onias II, either from his pro-Syrian leanings or from sheer incapacity, neglected to send the required 20 talents to Ptolemy Euergetes of Egypt. Such an act was close to rebellion and nearly led to the destruction of Judea. As it was, it resulted in the sale of the taxes to one Joseph, an adventurer of extraordinary boldness and ability, who became a sort of satrap in Judea and for twenty-two years held this position, mingling severity with liberality l so successfully that during the entire period the Jews were not only at peace with their neighbours, but reasonably prosperous in their internal affairs. The ultimate results, however, of this new departure in the administration of the state were not all so happy. Not only did it lead to civil strife, but the control of the taxes tended to concentrate wealth in the hands of Joseph and his sons and in those of the various agents they employed. There was thus formed a wealthy official class whose sympathies were increasingly with the Hellenistic culture discovered during their intercourse with the Egyptian court. Jewish society thus began more rapidly to feel those influences of Hellenism that were soon to play so tragic a role in its life influences that were strengthened by the unofficial relations existing between Palestine and the Jewish communities already flourishing in Alexandria and other Egyptian cities.

Such a responsible position as this of Joseph in itself implies a loss of prestige on the part of the high priest, but does not seem to involve any attempt at his humiliation or at the destruction of Judaism. Even, when after his victory over Antiochus III at Raphia (217 B.C.) Ptolemy IV (Philopator) entered into the temple at Jerusalem, he offered sacrifices, and his worst offence seems to have been that he forced his way into the Holy of Holies. At the battle of Banias (198 B.C.) Palestine fell wholly into the hands of Antiochus III and a brighter day seemed about to dawn. The Jews were kindly treated by their new ruler, who recognised their value as colonists and settled thousands of them in the various new cities which he founded. They were granted the right to live in accordance with their own laws, were relieved from a considerable portion of their taxes, while those of their number who were in slavery were allowed to return. This friendly legislation went so far as to make it a crime to carry into Jerusalem such meats as the Jews were forbidden to eat, while Seleucus IV is said to have borne all the costs of the sacrifices.

The failure of the attempt of Seleucus IV, through Heliodorus, to get possession of the temple treasures must have still further strengthened the position of the high priest. But this development was suddenly threatened, not alone by unaccustomed oppression on the part of Syria, but by the mistaken policy of the high priests themselves.

Under the Seleucid suzerains devotion to Hellenism became identified with loyalty. For there had grown up in Jerusalem a strong pro-Syrian party which sought political safety in complete dependence upon Syria. Its numbers were probably never large, but it embraced most of the prominent citizens of Jerusalem, and its position was strengthened by the fact that the high priest was now the king's appointee. This political sympathy was very naturally accompanied by a predilection for Greek culture and by a willingness to abandon Judaism as a cult. It might have been expected that the high priest would have strongly opposed these latter particulars, and it is true that under the administration of Onias III an effort was made to stem the latitudinarian movement, but with unfortunate results. The lines of cleavage along religious and political lines were so close together as not only to make the Syrian elements Hellenistic, but to make their opponents apparently loyal to Egypt. So bitter was the opposition to Onias on the part of the Syrian party notably on that of one Simon the Benjamite that he was forced to leave Jerusalem and for some time to live as a sort of exile-ambassador at Antioch. His absence aided the Hellenistic Syrian party, for not only was his brother Jason (or Jesus), who acted as his representative, a strong friend of Hellenism, but the irrepressible son of Joseph, Hyrcanus, whom Onias had befriended, complicated the situation by continuing to collect taxes for Egypt throughout the region on the east of Jordan commanded by his great castle.

It was while affairs were in this condition that Antiochus Epiphanes succeeded his brother Seleucus IV. Instantly the Hellenistic party grew stronger. Jason succeeded by large promises in getting Onias III removed and himself appointed as high priest. Antiochus Epiphanes, who had already determined upon the policy of religious conformity, willingly gave his consent. Jason was established as high priest. Then followed the extraordinary spectacle of a Jewish city undertaking to install a heathen civilisation, of priests abandoning their sacrifices, of Jewish youths exercising under Greek hats, and of a high priest sending 300 drachmas of silver to Tyre for a sacrifice to Hercules. Jason suffered the fate he had brought upon Onias, for after three years a Menelaus, the brother of Simon the Benjamite, offered Antiochus a larger bribe than had he, and was made high priest. Under his influence the process of Hellenising went on rapidly. Surgical operations removed traces of circumcision, and when Antiochus visited Jerusalem in 172 B.C., he was welcomed in Greek fashion, by a torchlight procession, and in every way was made to feel that his policy would prove successful and that it was only a matter of time before the Jews, like others of his dependent peoples, would have become fused in a Hellenistic mould.

This tendency to reverse the course of religious development was not merely an evidence of the rise of a political party and of personal ambition on the part of the high priests and the Gerousia. It resulted also from the general Hellenistic movement, which since the days of Alexander had begun to be felt throughout Palestine. Not alone into Alexandria and Asia Minor but also into Galilee and the country east of Jordan, did Greek as well as Jewish colonists press. Great centres of Greek trade grew up alongside of the smaller towns of the Jews. Even before the time of Alexander, Gaza had commercial relations with Greece, and Dora was probably subject to Athens. Ptolemy Philadelphia had favoured Greek colonisation in Judea, and, as if to offset this tendency, there had already begun the emigration that was to carry the Jews into all quarters of the known world. In Alexandria, thanks to the efforts of Alexander himself, as well as natural emigration, the Jews numbered hundreds of thousands. Fortunately, the influences they there felt were not those of the Hellenism that so often ruined the Eastern peoples, but rather those which sprang from the schools. By the end of the second century we find at least one Jewish philosopher, Aristobulus, and several poets, and at least a few years later, Jews held high political and military office under Egyptian rulers. But they chiefly shared in the Graeco-Egyptian intellectual life, and already there had begun that synthesis which was later to give the world Philo and the Kabbala. The Hebrew Scriptures were already translated into Greek, and religious writings had begun to appear in the same language. Thus, by their own kin in Egypt as well as by the heathen who ruled and surrounded them, the Jews of Palestine were being brought under the influence of an Orientalised Greek civilisation that rarely, if ever, failed to effect a change for the worse.

With Greek influences thus ubiquitous and persistent, it is not strange that men like Menelaus should have been eager to lead Judea out from its isolation into the circle of a more brilliant civilisation. They may not have desired utterly to abandon Jehovah, but they very clearly were eager to abandon the exclusiveness of the Jewish cult in search for a denationalised religion. Such a tendency might very easily have become an outright conversion to heathenism, but this, with necessary exceptions, a just allowance for the sympathies of Josephus and the two books of Maccabees, will hardly permit us to discover. Theirs was a religious indifferentism coupled with the enthusiasm of an abortive renaissance, but it was not idolatry.

The prostitution of the priesthood seems to have been endured within Jerusalem itself, whose inhabitants had been specially honoured by Antiochus III, and where the Syrian garrison made resistance futile; but when the report of the doings of Menelaus reached the outlying country, there was a general rising in the interest of decency and religion. The Gerousia itself sent messengers to Antiochus to prefer charges against the high priest. But all was in vain. Menelaus bribed the king, stole and sold some of the sacred vessels of the temple, and the wretched accusers paid the penalty of their temerity with their lives, as did also the aged Onias III, whom even the sanctuary of Apollo at Daphne did not protect.

But opposition to Hellenistic religion and culture had been developing, notwithstanding these successes of the high priest. Along with the drift of the priesthood toward Hellenism there ran a counter-current of legalistic orthodoxy the third great characteristic of the period. The members of the reactionary party were mostly scribes and their disciples, who, so far from desiring any share in Greek civilisation, opposed it fanatically. Historically this party represented Jewish spirit quite as truly as the priesthood. From the days of Ezra the genius of the nation had been growing scholastic. The study of the Thorah, though by no means reaching its later preeminence, was growing more intense and widespread. To men filled with the spirit of Moses and the prophets, the friends of heathen civilisation, priests though they might be, were "transgressors" and "lawless." Even articles made of glass, according to Jose ben Jochanan, were defiling, since they were made from Gentile soil. The true Jew was told, "Let thy house be a place of assembly for the wise; powder thyself with the dust of their feet," and every Sabbath, and indeed on other days, the Law was expounded in the synagogue by the professional teachers.

Under such inspiration the scribes and their followers slowly grew into a party that of the Chasidim, or "Pious." Scattered abroad over the little state, dwellers in small towns rather than in the capital, these earnest men and women studied and cherished the Thorah. Important as they were later to prove, both as a party and as the progenitors of parties, their lack of organisation, as well as their dispersion and poverty, weakened their influence in the state, and, as with all incipient popular reforms, conflict and persecution were needed to bring the movement to self-consciousness.

And in Judea there was developing between Hellenism and Judaism an irrepressible conflict that was destined to destroy the Hellenising influence of the aristocracy, give the nation a new dynasty and monarchy, reinstate an intense and uncompromising Judaism, and identify scribism with patriotism.

CHAPTER II: ANTIOCHUS EPIPHANES AND THE LOSS OF RELIGIOUS LIBERTY

THE dominance of the Hellenising party in church and state brought neither peace nor prosperity. Not only were the morals of the people degenerating, but the taxes levied by Syria were oppressive. Before the conquests of the Asmoneans the Jews were essentially an agricultural people, and, before the rise of the family of Joseph, included few, if any, rich men. In the absence of commerce, any considerable middle class could hardly have existed, and the nation as a whole seems to have been composed of fellaheen and aristocrats, priestly or professional. The two classes had different origins, different ambitions, and very possibly different languages. The supremacy of the Hellenistic elements of the aristocracy was, however, calculated to deepen the misery of the masses, since what little fellow-feeling there may have resulted from devotion to the law was of necessity lost.

Upon such a people the irresponsible rule of the Syrians sat heavily. As wealth was almost exclusively in lands and cattle, taxes were comparatively easy to collect, and of necessity fell with crushing weight upon the unfortunate fellaheen. What these taxes were can be seen from the various privileges granted or promised by Demetrius and other kings. They included a tax on the salt mined at the Dead Sea, a sum supposed to be equivalent to one-third the grain harvested and one-half the fruit, and, in addition, poll taxes and crown taxes, or sums equivalent to the value of crowns presented to the monarchs, as well as the temple tax of 10,000 drachmas. Further, Syrian officers had the right to seize cattle and stores for military purposes, as well as to enforce the corvee. When one recalls that all this was in addition to the tithes and gifts required of the people in support of their religion, it is not hard to realise the burden upon the people as a whole. Under Antiochus IV fiscal oppression was increasing, since his extravagance as well as the heavy demands of Rome, kept Syria always in need of new taxes. These were collected with a severity certainly not less than that shown previously by Joseph and later by Cassius, when persons and even cities, who could not meet the demands laid upon them, were sold into slavery.

Doubtless in part because of this wretched condition of their affairs, due to an irresponsible king and an unsympathetic local government, there arose a disaffection on the part of many Jews and a suspicion of the Jews on the part of the king.

In about 172 B.C. Antiochus became involved in a dispute with Egypt over the possession of Palestine, and war immediately broke out between the two nations, he himself acting on the offensive, and conducted one campaign each year between 171-68. In the second of these four campaigns he had conquered practically the whole of Egypt outside of Alexandria, when he suddenly started north, possibly because of the interference of Rome. As he came into Palestine he learned that Jason, whom, he had deposed, had shut up Menelaus in the citadel, and, although driven from the city, was at the head of a revolt. This news, coupled with his natural suspicion of the Egyptian leanings of the Judaistic party, caused him to march upon Jerusalem. He sacked the city, massacred or enslaved large numbers of its inhabitants, and, although he made no attack upon Judaism, with Menelaus as his guide he entered into the sanctuary, where he is said to have found a statue of Moses riding on an ass. He robbed the temple of its treasure, and carried off to Antioch the golden altar, the candlestick, the table of shewbread, the cups and sacred vessels, and even scaled off the gilt with which parts of the temple were overlaid. Then he left the city in the control of Menelaus, who was supported by Syrian officials and troops.

These acts of Antiochus Epiphanes were but the beginning of a desperate attempt to extirpate the anti-Hellenistic party. Such an attempt was, in a measure, due to the peculiarities of the king himself. Brave, generous, and to a considerable degree possessed of cultivated tastes, he was at the same time eccentric, passionate, and possessed of immeasurable self-conceit. Added to these personal elements were the suspected sympathies of the Chasidim with Egypt. But doubtless with even greater truth it may be ascribed to an unbalanced determination to consolidate and prolong the Syrian state by the establishment of a common civilisation. All should be one people. Had the already aggressive Hellenising movement been allowed to run its course among the Jews, it is not impossible (though, on the whole, in the light of Jewish history, not probable, since such heathen tendencies would most likely have produced a revival of prophetism) that Judaism, like other ethnic faiths, would have succumbed. But here the king's own character made patience out of the question and precipitated a struggle that was not to cease until the weak city-state was unexpectedly able to break free from a suddenly decadent empire, and the despised anti-Hellenistic party became supreme.

This new policy of Antiochus was inaugurated by an attack upon Jerusalem, and again the occasion of the attack lay in the king's Egyptian wars. In 168 B.C. he had all but conquered Egypt, when the Roman legate, Popilius, following the anti-Syrian policy which Rome then favoured, unexpectedly ordered him to return to Syria. Antiochus demanded time for deliberation. The Roman drew a circle about the king with his staff and ordered him to "deliberate there." The king deliberated and retreated!

But now more than ever did he see danger in having on his southern frontier an unassimilated nation like the Jews, among whom a strong anti-Syrian party might easily develop, if indeed it were not already in existence. He determined once and for all either to convert or exterminate those of their numbers whose devotion to Judaism argued disloyalty to Syria. Indeed, it is not impossible that for purely political reasons he planned to exterminate the Jews of Jerusalem as a whole, and to replace them by heathen colonists. With such a combination of purposes political, religious, and ambitious he got possession of Jerusalem by treachery, again sacked and burned it, plundered the temple, massacred many of the citizens, carried off ten thousand as slaves, threw down the walls, strengthened the acropolis until it was a citadel which completely commanded the temple and the city, and placed in it a strong Syrian garrison.

Again this was but a beginning. For the first time in the history of the Graeco-Roman world there began a war of extermination of a religion. Its victims were those who clung to Judaism, and above all the Pious. The observance of all Jewish rites, especially the Sabbath and circumcision, was punished by death. Jewish worship was abolished. Heathen altars were erected in all the cities of Judea, and in the temple groves were planted, and a small altar to Jupiter, the Abomination of Desolation, was erected upon the great altar of burnt-offering. There in December 168 B.C. a sow was sacrificed and the desecration was complete.

Then began the brief period of Jewish martyrs. Royal officers went about the land to see that the commands of the king were obeyed. But while many deserted their faith, and the Samaritans obtained by petition the right to erect a temple to Zeus upon Mt. Gerizim, the Chasidim and their sympathisers preferred death to denial. Old men and youths were whipped with rods and torn to pieces, mothers were crucified with the infant boys they had circumcised, strangled and hanging about their necks. To possess a copy of the law was to be punished by death. It would be hard to name a greater crisis in the history of the Jews, or indeed of any people. To compare it with the fortunes of the Low Countries during the reign of Philip II of Spain is to discredit neither brave little land.

But the persecution only intensified the devotion of the Chasidim to their Thorah. They were ready to die rather than surrender such few copies as they might own. Indeed, as later in the case of the Christians under Decius, persecution itself helped them to draw more clearly the distinction between their sacred books and those that were not worthy of supreme sacrifice; and during these dark days we may place the first beginning of that choice between religious books which afterward was to result in the fixing of the third group or stratum of books in the Hebrew Bible — "the Sacred Writings."

From the midst of this persecution, also, the hopes of the Pious leaped out in vision and prophecy. In the books of Daniel and Judith they pictured the deliverances wrought by Jehovah for those who kept his law in disobedience of some monstrous demand for universal idolatry, and traced the rise and fall of empires till the kingdom of the saints should come. Similar religious trust burst forth in lyric poetry, in which the misery of the land is painted no more vividly than the faith that the true Israel is the flock of Jehovah's pasture. Even more in the Visions of Enoch (Chs. 83-90) does the heart of a pious Israel find expression. To their unknown author the Chasidim were lambs killed and mutilated by fierce birds, while the apostate Jews looked on unmoved. But he saw deliverance as well. The Lord of the sheep should seat himself upon a throne "in a pleasant land," and cast the oppressors and the apostates into a fiery abyss; but the faithful martyrs should be brought to a new temple, and their eyes should be opened to see the good, and at last they should be like Messiah himself. For God would send his own anointed to his servants' aid, and he should found a new kingdom, not in heaven, but upon the earth. Indeed, if it be true that certain psalms belong to this period, these earnest souls from out of the depths of their sufferings proclaimed a Messianic time in which a revived and sanctified Israel would give the true religion to all the world.

Sustained by these bright visions — the seed of so much later Jewish hope — the Chasidim at first awaited Jehovah's time. They could die as martyrs, but they would not live as soldiers. But deliverance was to come by the sword, and events were to make this plain, even to the Chasidim. For out of this persecution arose the Judea of Judas Maccabaeus.

The misery of the land could not have continued long when, in accordance with the king's dragonnade, Appelles, a royal officer, came to Modein, a small town upon the hills of Judea overlooking the maritime plain. There he ordered all the inhabitants to a heathen sacrifice. Among those who answered his summons were Mattathias, the head of a priestly family supposedly descendants of one Chasinon or Asmon, and his five sons, John, Simon, Judas, Eleazar, and Jonathan. They were not members of the Chasidim but represented the wider circle of those whose devotion to the Law had been deeply stirred by the persecution. As Mattathias came to the little gathering the royal officer promised him a reward for conformity. Instantly the old priest with a great shout of protest killed the Jew who was attempting to offer a sacrifice, and his sons struck down the officer. Then, after levelling the altar with the ground, the entire family fled to the mountains. There they were joined by groups of the Chasidim, already fugitives, and by other men less religious but even more ready to oppose oppression. No sooner was the affair at Modein known than the Syrians undertook to punish the rebels, and the fanatical devotion of some of the Chasidim to the Sabbath for a time threatened disaster. On one occasion a group allowed themselves to be slaughtered by the Syrians rather than break the Sabbath defending themselves. But the strong common sense of Mattathias convinced even these zealots that such devotion was ill-advised, and other bands of the Pious submitted to the stern necessities that were laid upon religion. Then, with his troop of fanatical, undisciplined, and ill-armed followers, Mattathias began a religious war. Up and down Judea the wild troops ranged, avoiding the larger cities, hiding by day, attacking by night, "smiting sinners in their anger and lawless men in their wrath," pulling down heathen altars, forcibly circumcising children, pursuing after the "sons of pride," and, as far as they were able, guaranteeing safety in the observance of the Law.

For perhaps a year the old man was able to maintain this rough life, and then he died (166 B.C.), urging his sons to "recompense fully the heathen and to regard the commandments of the Law." The conduct of the struggle he bequeathed to Judas, his third son, but recommended Simon as a counsellor. His followers buried him in the family tomb at Modein, and prepared for the greater struggle which was clearly before them.

CHAPTER III: JUDAS MACCABEUS AND THE REESTABLISHMENT OF RELIGIOUS LIBERTY (165-161 B.C.)

THE condition of Judea when thus Judas succeeded to the captaincy of a religious guerilla war was briefly this: On the one side, the legitimate political powers, the high priest and the Syrian captain-general, together with a considerable number of the more aristocratic citizens, were united in the endeavour to force the nation into submission to Syria and into conformity with the religion of the rest of the known world. On the other, was a force of insurgents under Judas, made up of two very different groups of men, — the fanatical Chasidim, and the patriotic adventurers constituting the party of the Asmoneans or Maccabees. Between these two parties in the approaching civil war was the great mass of the people, doubtless at heart favourable toward Judaism, but indifferent to calls to heroic sacrifice, poor and unarmed, certain to be oppressed whichever side won, and consequently ready to submit to whichever party might for the moment be the victor. To speak of an uprising of the people is as misleading as in the case of England during the wars of the Roses.

Judas the Hammer — for such seems to be the most likely meaning of his title — is the ideal of the writer of 1 Maccabees — "a lion in his deeds, and a lion's whelp roaring for prey." And it must be confessed that not even Scotland can boast of a more typical border patriot, or one who better combined foresight with recklessness, genuine military ability with personal daring.

Desperate as the position of the rebels really was, the uprising at its beginning met with great good fortune. Apollonius, the commander of the Syrian forces in Judea and Samaria, was completely defeated and he himself was killed, Judas thereafter wearing his sword. Shortly afterward Seron, perhaps the commander of the Syrian forces in the maritime plain, attempted to punish Judas and came up toward Jerusalem by the way of the Beth-horons. But Judas never faltered. Appealing to his followers to remember their families and their laws, he rushed down upon the Syrians as they were crowded into a narrow defile, routed them, and pursued them into the plain with great slaughter.

Meanwhile the finances of Syria had grown so desperately bad that Antiochus undertook an expedition against the Persians to collect overdue tribute. He therefore divided his forces, giving one-half to Lysias, of the blood royal, whom he made governor-general of the region between the Euphrates and Egypt. Lysias was to despatch at once a large force against Judas, to drive out the Jews, and divide their land among colonists.

Lysias put three generals — Ptolemy, Nicanor, and Gorgias — in charge of the army of invasion and sent them southward, so confident of victory that slave-dealers accompanied them in anticipation of a vast supply of captives. Apparently the purpose of Antiochus was no longer to hellenise but to exterminate the Jews as a nation.

The news of the approach of this large force brought dismay to the Jews, but at the call of Judas large of numbers of them gathered at Mizpeh, the ancient sanctuary. There they fasted, put on sackcloth and ashes, and over their ancient scriptures, upon which the persecutors had drawn images of their idols, they prayed and offered the gifts which were properly the dues of the priests. Sending away all those excused from military duty by the Law, as well as all others who might be tempted to flee, Judas organised those that were left by appointing leaders of thousands and hundreds and fifties. Thus prepared he waited upon the south side of Emmaus, near which the Syrians had also camped. Each army attempted to surprise the other by night. Gorgias, with a force of five thousand infantry and a thousand horse, succeeded in reaching the camp of Judas, but only to find it deserted. For Judas, perceiving the movement, had simultaneously marched upon the Syrians. At daybreak he fell upon them, utterly defeated them, and pursued them to Gazara, Azotus, and Jamnia. Returning to the captured camp, the Jews, without stopping to plunder it, waited for the return of Gorgias. When that general appeared and saw his camp in flames and the Jews drawn up ready for attack, he at once retreated to the Philistine cities, while the Jews passed the Sabbath in celebration and thanksgiving.

Yet Judas did not feel himself strong enough to retake Jerusalem, if indeed there were not other forces of Syrians to be driven from the land. It was not till the next year (165 B.C.), however, that Lysias came with another huge army; but instead of coming into Judea from the north or west, he made a detour and came up through Idumea and the broad wady commanded by Bethzur, twenty miles south of Jerusalem on the road to Hebron. There Judas met him with a force of ten thousand men and won a decisive victory. Lysias retreated to Antioch to raise new forces, and as the Syrian garrisons scattered over the land were too weak to face Judas and his veterans, the land was momentarily free.

Then it was that the real purpose of the revolt could be accomplished. Fresh from its victory at Bethzur, the army went to Jerusalem to restore the temple. A detachment was sent to fight against the garrison in the citadel, while, amidst great lamentation over the burned gates and profaned courts and altar, Judas appointed such priests as had not yielded to the Hellenistic madness to cleanse the holy building and to throw all polluted stones into "an unclean place" — possibly the valley of Hinnom. At the ancient altar of burnt offering they hesitated. It had been polluted, but it was still sacred. It could neither be used nor thrown away, and in their uncertainty they took it solemnly apart and stored its unhewn stones in one of the chambers of the inner court, just off holy ground, where they might rest until some prophet should come who could decide as to their final destination. Then they erected a new altar that reproduced the old, rebuilt the dilapidated temple, rooted up the groves in the courts, made new temple furniture, restored the candlestick, the altar of incense, and the table for the shewbread. At last there came the day when incense burned again upon the altar, the lamps were relighted, the great curtains were rehung. As the dawn broke on the next morning, the 25th of Chisleu, 165, three years to a day since its predecessor had been desecrated, sacrifice was offered upon the great altar, and during eight days of delirious rejoicing the people again consecrated the great area to Jehovah. From that day to this the Feast of the Dedication — or the Feast of Lights — has been celebrated.

But the Jews had not achieved independence. They had simply regained an opportunity for worshipping Jehovah. The Syrian garrison still overlooked the temple from Akra, and political independence was probably not wanted by the people as a whole. One thing only was certain: now that the temple had been reconsecrated, no Syrian should be permitted again to seize the capital. The plans of Judas were more far-reaching than the mere maintenance of the position thus far gained, and he strengthened the city's walls, built huge towers, refortified Beth-zur on the southern frontier and garrisoned it with Jewish troops. The marauding Arabs on the frontier were taught respect for the new power. The Idumeans were defeated at Akrabattene, the otherwise unknown Balanites were burned alive in their own towers, while their Greek general, Timotheus, was unable to save the Ammonites from utter defeat and the loss of Jazer with its villages.

As happened again in the fearful year 66 A.D., the report of the Jews' uprising and these successes stirred to madness the neighbouring heathen regions into which the Jews had pushed. The inhabitants of Gilead undertook to exterminate the Jews living east of Jordan. At the same time appeals came from the Jewish colonists in Galilee for protection against expeditions being formed in Ptolemais and other Syrian cities. Judaism was in danger throughout the land. Judas acted promptly. Simon and three thousand men were sent to bring the Jews from Galilee, while Judas and Jonathan with eight thousand men went into Gilead. The rest of the army was left to defend Jerusalem and maintain order.

Both of the expeditions were successful. Simon, after considerable fighting, rescued the Galilean Jews and brought them to safety in Judea. Judas, by swift marches, on the fifth day surprised the enemy just as they were attacking the last refuge of the Jews east of Judea, defeated them, burned several of their cities, and at Raphana — that lost city of the Decapolis — destroyed a confederacy organised by one Timotheus, and burned the fugitives together with the temple in which they had taken refuge. But his position was too precarious to allow the raid to lead into conquest. Gathering all the Jews together he forced his way with them through the city Ephron, which attempted to shut him out from the roads and fords it commanded, and at last brought them amidst great rejoicing to Jerusalem and safety.

There he was forced to make good losses caused by the reckless disobedience of his lieutenants, and then destroyed Hebron, and Azotus with its altars and its gods. Then he began a siege of the citadel (163-162 B.C.). But the people, especially the Chasidim, had had enough of fighting. They had regained the temple and were content. Almost at this moment, also, Syria was able to deal vigorously with the revolt. Antiochus Epiphanes, who had found little wealth among the Persians, had died (164 B.C.), after a vain attempt to rob a rich temple in Elymais, overcome — as the writer of 1 Maccabees believed — by grief for the reverses he had suffered in Judea. On his death-bed, instead of confirming Lysias as guardian of the young Antiochus V — a post he already exercised — he appointed one Philip to the office. None the less Lysias refused to submit, and proclaiming his ward king, ruled as regent.

Under these circumstances the aristocratic party, whom Judas had hunted up and down Judea and had at last shut up in Akra, found it easy to interest Lysias in the further designs of the Asmoneans, and the regent at once made preparations for a new invasion of Judea. Again he approached Jerusalem from the south. Beth-zur was threatened and Judas was forced to raise his siege of Akra to march to its relief. He met the Syrians near Beth-Zacharias. His troops fought desperately, his brother Eleazar being crushed to death under the elephant he had stabbed in hopes of dismounting and killing the young Antiochus. But all was to no purpose. The little force of the Jews was beaten back into Jerusalem. Beth-zur received a Syrian garrison, Judas retreated to the mountains, and Jerusalem itself was immediately besieged.

It was the sabbatical year, and the influx of refugees from Galilee and Gilead had seriously diminished the provisions of the city. The Syrians had siege artillery, while the Jews had none except that improvised during the siege. Altogether it is easy to see that the inevitable outcome of the siege must have been the fall of the city. But, as at other times, such a misfortune was providentially prevented. Lysias heard that Philip was marching against him, and seeing that it was impossible for the Jewish aristocracy to force the people into Hellenistic customs, offered religious liberty in return for political submission. The Chasidim accepted the terms, and upon the surrender of the city the nation was solemnly given the right to live according to its own laws. The inquisition of Antiochus Epiphanes was abolished, and that for which the Chasidim and Mattathias had risen was accomplished. And if, as Josephus says, Lysias killed the high priest Menelaus, who had held the office throughout these unhappy years, the pious Jew would have seen in the act no insult to Jehovah, but a new evidence of divine retribution.

With this charter of Lysias began a new era in the Maccabean house. Hitherto they had stood for the hopes of the best and most pious element of their nation; now that religious liberty was assured, their position was anomalous. Neither high priest nor a representative of Syria, it seemed to many Jews as if Judas should cease to head a revolt and should retire again to the quiet of Modein.

But Judas was no Cincinnatus. A religious war might indeed no longer be possible, but political independence was something that might still be hoped and battled for. If the earlier battles had been for the Law, the new should be for fatherland; and so it was that he did not disband his forces but kept them under arms, becoming at once an outlaw, the head of insurrection and the centre of whatever nationalist feeling the land contained. Immediately the Chasidim deserted him. They cared nothing for politics, and had gained all they had demanded; and when, after Philip, Lysias, and little Antiochus V had each been killed, Demetrius I appointed the priest Alcimus as the successor of the renegade Menelaus, the Chasidim received him heartily. Hellenist though he was, he was of the seed of Aaron and would do them no harm.

With Alcimus came the Syrian general Bacchides with a considerable force for the purpose of completing the reduction of the nation and of killing Judas. He met but little opposition, and after wantonly killing a few of the Jews, doubtless Chasidim, who had surrendered to him, returned to Antioch, leaving Alcimus as the head of the state, supported by Syrian troops. Between the high priest and Judas there immediately sprang up a civil war, in which Judas was apparently the more successful. Alcimus called upon Demetrius I for aid. The king replied by sending his friend Nicanor with a large army against Judas. After suffering a check at Capharsalama, in the vicinity of Lydda, Nicanor came into Jerusalem. There he completely lost all the advantages won for the Hellenistic party by Bacchides. In utter disregard of the needs of the crisis, he not only attempted to imprison prominent members of the Chasidim, but threatened to destroy the temple if Judas was not delivered into his hands. Such a threat turned the Chasidim back to their old champion. Religious liberty was in danger, and all Judea streamed to Judas.

At the beginning of March Nicanor met Judas at Adasa, a town near the Beth-horons. The battle was fought desperately, but Judas won. Nicanor was killed, and before night his head and right hand were hanging upon the fortifications of Jerusalem. The day was set apart as a festival (thirteenth of Adar), and as Nicanor's Day was celebrated for centuries.

Again Judas was supported by all thorough Jews, and again he undertook to crush heathenism and build up a Jewish state. But he also sent an embassy to Rome, already a power in Syrian politics. So successful was he that he not only made an offensive and defensive alliance with the republic, but induced Rome to threaten Demetrius I with war, unless he immediately left the Jews in peace. Unfortunately, however, this decree arrived too late to prevent the catastrophe which was approaching.

For the position of Judas during those few weeks in which he was head of the little state was again that of a military dictator, unconstitutional, and wholly dependent upon the success of his troop of half-professional soldiers. High priest or Syrian governor he was not, for Alcimus still lived, to return with Bacchides, a sort of legitimist seeking the overthrow of a miniature Napoleon.

The new invasion was undertaken by Demetrius, to avenge the death of Nicanor, before any message could arrive from Rome. His force consisted of twenty thousand infantry and two thousand cavalry under Bacchides. Two months after the death of Nicanor this army had marched south, and, about Passover time, encamped against Jerusalem, from which they soon removed to Berea to meet Judas, who was at Alasa. The position of Judas as a revolutionary chief, no longer fighting for religion, but opposed to the high priest, at once grew weak. His embassy to Rome, prudent as it was, injured him. The Chasidim, fearing foreign entanglements, were again unwilling to carry on the war, and the battle was simply between the Syrians and the Asmoneans for the control of Judea. Into such a struggle, stripped of national issues, few would follow Judas, and his army deserted him until he had at his command only eight hundred men. Against their advice he determined upon battle, and charged the enemy with a handful of his most desperate followers. For a moment he was successful. He broke through and routed the right wing of the Syrian army under the command of Bacchides himself. But it was of no avail. The Syrian left wing swung around upon him, his troops were killed or put to flight, and Judas himself fell.

After the battle his two brothers, Simon and Jonathan, were permitted to bury his body at Modein.

The brief heroic age of the Maccabean struggle was ended. The little state passed again — though with religious liberty assured — under the high priest and the Syrian legate, and the party of Judas became again a band of outlaws. But Judas had not lived in vain. The Jewish faith had been saved, and the Chasidim had been taught their power. He had founded a family and a following that were to play a large role in the next century and more of Jewish history, and he had awakened a genuinely Jewish ambition and enthusiasm. But perhaps as much as anything, he had given Judaism a hero, in devotion and bravery fit to be compared with David himself.

CHAPTER IV: JONATHAN AND THE BEGINNINGS OF NATIONALITY (161-143 B.C.)

THE death of Judas was the signal for the members of the Hellenistic party, whom his fierce administration had forced into hiding, to "put forth their heads" and to join exultantly with Alcimus in searching out the followers of the dead leader. Yet the work of Judas was not altogether lost, and in the face of the ruin that had overtaken them, his friends ventured to call upon his brother Jonathan, rightly surnamed Apphus, "the wary," to succeed to the leadership of their forlorn hope.

The first exploits of the new chief were of no political significance. He was an outlaw at the head of a band — or comitatus — of outlaws. To escape from Bacchides, he made his camp in the stretch of desolate mountainous pasturage of Tekoah, between Bethlehem and the Dead Sea. As it soon became evident that they would there be exposed to the attacks of Bacchides, Jonathan sent his baggage in charge of his brother John across Jordan, into the land of the Nabateans who had given Judas proof of their friendship. But the tribe of Jambri, living in Medaba, attacked the train and killed John. Thereupon Jonathan and Simon crossed the Jordan to avenge their brother. They fell upon the Jambri as they were celebrating a wedding, slaughtered and plundered to their satisfaction, and then turned homeward, only to find themselves hemmed in by the Syrian forces, between the river and its marshes. Thereupon abandoning their camp and baggage, the entire troop swam the Jordan and again found refuge in the wilderness of Judea.

Bacchides followed up the success by a systematic attempt at controlling Judea. The towns commanding the ways leading to Jerusalem, Jericho, Emmaus, Beth-horon, Bethel, together with Timnath, Pharathon, and Tephon, were fortified and garrisoned, while the fortifications of Beth-zur, Gazara and the citadel of Jerusalem were strengthened. The sons of the leading men of the towns were sent to Jerusalem to be held as hostages in the citadel. Alcimus, although not a violent Hellenist, in the meantime was endeavouring to obliterate the distinction between Jews and Gentiles by tearing down the soreg, or high wall, that divided the court of one from the court of the other in the temple area — a piece of profanation that, in the eyes of the Pious, was punished by his death in torments shortly after the work of destruction had begun.

Under these circumstances, with the disappearance of civil war and the apparent destruction of the Asmonean party, Bacchides judged the country to be at peace and returned to Syria, and in the pregnant words of 1 Maccabees, "the land had rest two years." In truth, the fortunes of the Asmonean house had never been at so low an ebb. Their movement had been repudiated by their old friends the Chasidim, now more than ever seen to be not a political but an ecclesiastical party, the Hellenistic party was again in control of the state, the high-priesthood was vacant; the entire land was covered by Syrian garrisons; while they themselves, after having been decisively defeated, were reduced to a small band hiding in the wilderness. Yet their fortune was suddenly to turn. It can hardly be that the plans of Jonathan were those of a nationalist, in the modern sense of the word, for of a nation in his time there was no thought. At the best he can have regarded his own elevation to political power as a part of the divine plan for his people. But whatever his motive, his preparations were made so quietly that the Syrian sympathisers were deceived, and thought that the opportunity had come to seize him. They thereupon asked Demetrius to make the attempt. The king again sent Bacchides, who at once sought by fair means or foul to get possession of Jonathan. Failing in this, he besieged Jonathan and Simon in their fortified town of Bethbasi. The siege, however, was anything but successful, and Bacchides was persuaded to agree to a treaty, according to which Jonathan was relieved from all further danger of attack, and allowed to live in Michmash (153 B.C.) as a sort of licensed freebooter, free from the fear of the Syrians. There, like David at Hebron, he governed such of the people as he could, raided the surrounding country, "destroyed the ungodly," and by degrees made himself the most powerful element of the troubled little state. He was, however, a revolutionary ruler; for the constitutional authority, the Syrian Governor, was still in possession of the citadel and city of Jerusalem, and as there was no high priest appointed after the death of Alcimus, it is certain that Jonathan did not enjoy this honour. Yet such were the political conditions of Judea at the time of his establishment at Michmash, and so troubled were the affairs of Syria, that a shrewd man like Jonathan had little difficulty in manipulating politics in such a way as practically to free himself from any real control.

Alexander Balas, a young man of mean origin, was put forward by Attalus, king of Pergamum, and other enemies of Demetrius I, as the son and heir of Antiochus Epiphanes. So strong was his support that the empire was thrown into civil war. In this war the friendship and support of Jonathan were essential to each party, and both Alexander and Demetrius began to bid for his aid. Demetrius promised Jonathan the right to raise and maintain an army, and the return of all hostages. Armed with these new powers, Jonathan abandoned his headquarters at Michmash and went to Jerusalem, where he established himself, rebuilding the walls and repairing the city, but not driving out the Syrian garrison in the citadel. The garrisons, however, established by Bacchides in the outlying towns, with the exception of that in Beth-zur, all fled to Syria.

But even greater changes were at hand. Hearing of the offers of Demetrius, Alexander appointed Jonathan high priest, made him one of his "friends" and, as a token of his new princely rank, sent him a purple robe and a golden crown, all of which, with fine disregard of his alliance with Demetrius, Jonathan accepted. At the Feast of Tabernacles, 153 B.C., seven years after the death of Alcimus, Jonathan officiated for the first time at the altar. Wholly by the will of the Syrians, the outlaw of Tekoa, the licensed rebel of Michmash, had become the legal head of Judea, and the Maccabean movement had become identified with Judaism.

The importance of this fact is great. Prom this time Jonathan and the Maccabean house could rely upon the loyalty of the Chasidim, for the rapidly developing party of the Scribes could not desert a warrior who was the high priest. The fact that he was not of the family of Zadok injured him, in their eyes, no more than it had Alcimus. Like that latitudinarian, "he was of the family of Aaron, and could do them no harm." Equally harmless was the sincere but quixotic attempt of Onias, the son of the orthodox Onias III, to offset the transfer of the sacred office to Alcimus by establishing (160 B.C.) himself as a sort of "legitimate" high priest over a small temple at Leontopolis, near Hieropolis in Egypt. Thanks to the favour of Ptolemy Philometor, the temple was indeed constructed from a ruined stronghold or heathen temple, sacred vessels of unusual shape were installed within it, the necessary funds were furnished from the royal treasury, and Onias was established as high priest over Levites and priests. But notwithstanding it was supposed to fulfil a prophecy of Isaiah, this counterfeit sanctuary never attained any great importance, and least of all in the days of Jonathan.

Not to be outdone by his rival, Demetrius not only recognised Jonathan as high priest, but promised the most extravagant favours and privileges the remission of the poll tax, the salt tax, the tax on grain and fruits, the exemption of Jerusalem from all taxes, the cession of the citadel, the return of all Jewish captives and slaves, the appropriation of 150,000 drachmas to the temple. Whether or not Jonathan accepted such terms, which the king if successful could hardly have been expected to fulfil, is not stated by our sources. In the light of Jonathan's usual clear foresight it is unlikely, and when Demetrius I was finally defeated and killed by Alexander (150 B. C.), it is probable that Jonathan's troops shared in the victory.

When Balas in turn was threatened by the son of Demetrius (Demetrius II), Jonathan seized the opportunity to extend his territory to the sea. Accepting a challenge of Apollonius, the governor of Coele-Syria, who had gone over to Demetrius II, he marched from Jerusalem at the head of ten thousand picked troops and appeared before Joppa. The Syrian garrison attempted resistance, but the gates were opened by the citizens, and the city fell into Jonathan's hands. The Jews thus got possession of the natural seaport of Jerusalem, and despite its subsequent vicissitudes Joppa remained henceforth a Jewish city of the most pronounced type.

After this success Jonathan defeated Apollonius near Azotus (Ashdod), took the city and burned it, and then shut up a great number of fugitives in the temple of Dagon, and burned it and them. Thence he proceeded to Askelon, which surrendered without battle, and he returned to Jerusalem loaded with booty. In all of these exploits the high priest acted as an officer of Alexander, and as a reward for his services was presented by the pretender with a gold buckle (an honour equivalent to an admission of semi-independent vassalage), and given Ekron with its surrounding country. When, subsequently (147 B.C.), Alexander, defeated as much by his own foolish government as by his enemies, fled from his kingdom only to die by assassination, Jonathan exploited the misfortunes of Syria to the utmost. Demetrius II, who came thus unexpectedly to the throne (146-145 B.C.), was in no position to force the Jews into submission, and Jonathan proceeded to besiege the citadel in Jerusalem. Whatever political ambitions on his part such an attempt implies, it is clear that he was by no means free from the Syrian suzerainty, for the Hellenists hastened to report the new uprising to the Syrian court. The news angered Demetrius, and he immediately started south, ordering Jonathan to raise the siege and meet him at Ptolemais. Instead of obeying the first command, Jonathan left his forces still engaged in the siege, and, with a company of priests and a large supply of presents, went to Demetrius and so won him over that, instead of being punished for the acts with which his enemies proceeded to charge him, he was named one of the king's chief friends, confirmed in the high-priesthood and in all his other honours, offices, and possessions, including the three Samaritan toparchies (Apperima, Lydda, and Eamat), and in return for 300 talents succeeded in getting all Jews freed from tribute in fact, gained nearly all the privileges promised him by Demetrius I.

A short time later circumstances again favoured Jonathan. A revolt broke out in Antioch, which Demetrius, thanks to ill-advised economy, could not put down. In despair he called upon Jonathan for aid. It was given on the express condition that the Syrian garrison should be removed from the citadel. With the aid of Jonathan's troops Demetrius succeeded in crushing the revolt of his citizens, but once in safety, with the usual treachery of his house, he refused to withdraw the garrison, and even threatened Jonathan with war unless he paid the tribute from which he had but just been relieved. But the nationalist movement was now too strong both in military resources and religious prestige for such threats to do more than increase its strength. Jonathan transferred his allegiance to the young Antiochus (VI), whom Trypho had caused to be crowned, and again had his various honours and privileges confirmed. In addition, his brother Simon was made military commander of the non-Judean country from the Ladder of Tyre to Egypt. Thus raised to unexpected military influence, the two brothers immediately proceeded to secure their territories for their new monarch, and incidentally to advance their own political independence. They forced Ascalon and Gaza to swear allegiance to Antiochus and to give hostages. These, however, Jonathan sent not to Antioch but to Jerusalem — a fact that indicates how independent he already regarded his position. Shortly after, hearing that Demetrius was moving upon him through Galilee, Jonathan marched against him, leaving Simon to complete the subjection of Beth-zur. Near Hazor the Jews fell into an ambush and fled in panic. Jonathan, however, succeeded in rallying them and completely defeated the enemy. The only relics of Syrian power now left in Judea were the garrisons in the citadel of Jerusalem and in Gazara,

As in the case of Judas, the situation of Jonathan, at once successful and critical, led to an attempt to form foreign alliances. Though nominally an officer (ethnarch of the Jews) under the crown, he acted as an independent ruler. Numenius and Antipater were sent to Rome to renew the treaty made by Judas, and what is at first sight somewhat surprising, they also took letters from "Jonathan the high priest, and the senate of the nation, and the priests and the rest of the people" to "their brethren, the Spartans," in order to renew a treaty made under Onias I. What was the result of this embassy we cannot say, but at all events it did not prevent (144 B.C.) preparations for another invasion of Palestine by Demetrius. Jonathan anticipated the attack, marched to the north, and at Hamath so terrified the Syrians that they fled without a battle. He pursued them as far as the Eleutherus, the boundary of Syria, and then turning eastward plundered the Zabadeans who lived on the sides of Anti-Lebanon, and marched upon Damascus, which was already at least nominally under his control as a representative of Antiochus VI and Trypho. In the meantime Simon was conquering the cities of the maritime plain and garrisoning Joppa. Returning from the north, Jonathan strengthened the fortifications of Jerusalem and, with the advice of the Gerousia, began a wall that would quite cut off the citadel from the surrounding country. He also fortified Adida which controlled the road between Jerusalem and Joppa. From being a high priest freed from tribute, the head of a veteran army, the captain-general of Syria, and the ethnarch of his people, it was but a short step to becoming a high priest, the head of an independent people.

Nor was his purpose unobserved. Trypho was unwilling that the Jewish people should thus become independent, and at the head of a large force marched on Jerusalem. At Bethshean Jonathan met him at the head of the largest army the state had yet produced. Unwilling to risk an open battle, Trypho used treachery. Under pretence of friendship he induced Jonathan to go to Ptolemais with only a small bodyguard. No sooner had Jonathan entered the city than the gates were closed, his men were slaughtered, and he was made a prisoner. Having thus his opponent in his power, Trypho at once undertook to destroy the Jewish forces near Bethshean, but though without their leader the soldiers prepared for battle and faced the Syrians so resolutely that Trypho fell back, probably upon Ptolemais. The Jewish troops thereupon returned to Judea unmolested and prepared for the worst their heathen neighbours could prepare. With both of the rival kings of Syria its enemies, with the Greek cities threatening war, with its leader a captive in the hands of the Syrians, the little state saw little in its future but destruction.

CHAPTER V: SIMON AND THE CONSOLIDATION OF JUDAISM (143-135 B.C.)

IN full confidence of a speedy victory over a discouraged and disorganised people, Trypho marched from Ptolemais, carrying with him the unfortunate Jonathan as his prisoner. His route led him south through the maritime plain and then east by Adida toward Jerusalem. But at Adida he met Simon, who had gathered troops at his own expense and had voluntarily assumed the leadership of Judea. Trypho did not wish a battle here any more than at Bethshean. To fall back was dangerous, since Simon had already seized Joppa. Yet he forced Simon to give him 100 talents of silver together with two of Jonathan's sons, on the promise that the high priest should be released on these terms. But after Simon had performed his part of the contract Trypho refused to release Jonathan and moved south along the Shephelah, apparently intending to come upon Jerusalem by the way of Idumea and Hebron. Simon moved along the hills parallel to the invader, a Jewish Fabius. Prevented by a snowstorm from forcing the southern approach to Jerusalem, Trypho marched around the southern end of the Dead Sea into Gilead, and there, at an unidentified town, Bascama, he killed Jonathan and went back to Syria. There he caused the boy king, Antiochus VI, to be killed, and reigned in name as well as power. Some time afterward Simon took the bones of his brother to Modein and buried them by the side of his father and his brothers, erecting a large monument and seven pyramids in honour of his family.

It was to be Simon's good fortune, without performing great exploits, to break still more the political dependence of Judea upon Syria and thus to enable Judaism, both outwardly and inwardly, to advance another stage in its evolution. Throughout the quarter of a century of struggle he had borne his share of dangers and anxieties from the time that the dying Mattathias had bidden the four brothers listen to him as their counsellor. As it was, the order of the three men's leadership was fortunate. In the days of Judas military daring was the one thing the oppressed nation wanted; in Jonathan's days, a mixture of military daring with more or less unscrupulous diplomacy; but in the days of Simon a man was required who should not only be ready to fight and intrigue, but should also be able to hold foreign politics in equilibrium while he was reconstructing the Jewish state, preparing the way for political independence, and, what was of especial importance, developing a party upon whom his house could rely for support.

It was in this latter particular that the administration of Simon was to be of significance to Jewish history. Hitherto the Jews had been broken roughly into the Hellenist, the Chasidim, and the Maccabean parties. The assumption of the high-priesthood by the Maccabees had momentarily fused the two latter into a religio-nationalist party, which, thanks to its success in dealing with Syria as well as its severity with all Syrian sympathisers, had become the dominant force in the state.

But the fusion that gave rise to this party never destroyed the identity or character of its two constituents, and as the pressure of foreign danger weakened each began to reassert itself. On the one hand, there were those who favoured a narrow religio-political policy, and on the other those who wished to see the Jews a nation among nations. The spirit of the former party was that of Chasidim and scribism, and it was to develop into Pharisaism. The spirit of the other was the last relic of sympathy with Hellenistic culture and was to mark the Sadducees. Accurately speaking, the Maccabean dynasty belonged to neither party, but used each in turn. Judea was to taste the bitter and sweet of national politics, in which a family, supreme in religion as well as in administration, was to carry through an hereditary policy by the aid now of one and now of the other of two rivals.

It was no small danger that confronted Simon at the murder of Jonathan, though by no means so desperate as that occasioned by the death of Judas. If, indeed, his brother had been killed, and if he himself was confronted by an arrogant king backed by a powerful army, he was the constitutional head of a nation, no longer poverty-stricken, but possessed of military resources and prestige. Quite as important was the struggle between Demetrius and Trypho, which enabled him to strengthen and provision his fortresses in Judea. At last the excesses of Trypho's soldiers led Simon to send an embassy to Demetrius II with rich presents and to propose an alliance against their common enemy, as well as an adjustment of the tribute. In this he was completely successful. Demetrius granted pardon for all of the Jews' doings, confirmed them in their possession of the strongholds they had built (although no mention is made of Joppa and the other cities Jonathan and Simon had captured), and remitted all tributes.

Thus, to quote the exultant words of 1 Maccabees, "was the yoke of the heathen taken away from Israel" (143-42 B.C.).

From this time the Jews began to reckon in their own cycle, the first year of which would thus correspond with 170 of the Seleucid. Documents and contracts were now dated according to the year of Simon, although the Seleucid cycle was used parallel. As a further proof of his practical independence Simon now began to issue coins bearing on one side Holy Jerusalem, or Jerusalem the Holy, and on the other, the word "shekel" or "half shekel." Each bore the year of coinage, probably of the cycle of Jerusalem rather than of Simon's reign.

Although it is not expressly stated, it is altogether probable that even before this time Simon had officiated as high priest, for as such Demetrius II recognises him. But the hereditary right of his family, not yet recognised, was now to be formally fixed. The influence of the Chasidim and scribes is here very evident, as well as the thoroughly religious character of Simon's administration. Shortly after the retreat of Trypho Simon had captured Gazara, driven out its heathen inhabitants, and colonised it with "men who observed the Law." Almost at the same time the Syrian garrison in Jerusalem had been starved into surrender and allowed to leave the country. Thus, a quarter of a century after the beginning of their struggle (May, 142 B.C.) the people of Jerusalem celebrated their deliverance from the hated guard with the same enthusiasm as that with which their fathers, under Judas, had celebrated the cleansing of the temple. The citadel was purified and held as a stronghold, while Simon also erected a palace for himself on the opposite mount. Then the Jewish people (September, 141), priests, people, princes of the people, and elders of the land, in gratitude for his great services, chose Simon high priest, general, and ethnarch, "forever, until there should arise a faithful prophet." Except him no priest was to gather an assembly or wear a badge of supreme authority, and his word was final as regarded the sanctuary and the state. Thus, by no decision of a Syrian king, but by the Jewish people itself, greater authority than had been the high priest's before the days of Antiochus Epiphanes was settled upon a new family. A military state had become an hereditary theocracy. The chief of outlaws had become a high priest forever after the order of Melchizedek.

Yet in one particular the new dynasty gives possible evidence of the beginning of a nation. Simon, as his coins show, was at the head of a city, but in the "great congregation" that shared in the establishment of the new high-priestly family one can see the uncertain rise of the people as against the first estate of the priests.

And another important change is to be seen. From the days of Joseph, the son of Tobias, who had been a fiscal if not a civil official in Judea, by the side of the high priest, there had been in Jerusalem some special representative of the Syrian control, like Apollonius or Bacchides. But now this Syrian official disappeared and the civil authority was vested in Simon as ethnarch, just as the military and religious powers were his, by virtue of his being high priest and military governor. With so much power vested in his hands, both by the vote of the people and the act of the Syrian king, Simon was but little short of an independent ruler.

Yet, singularly enough, we know but little of the years of prosperity that followed the inauguration of the new house, but all information that we can recover evidences that prosperity, in which "the ancient men sat in the streets," "the young men put on glorious and warlike apparel," and "they sat each man under his vine and his fig tree, and there was none to make them afraid." The most rigid Judaism prospered. Heathen were exterminated with a relentlessness worthy of Antiochus Epiphanes. Sorcerers were hanged in companies. The temple was filled with new and magnificent utensils, and its service enriched with new collections of Psalms, in which the triumphant nationalism burst out in thanksgiving to Jehovah and glorification of the new dynasty. And, if there was no prophet in the land, there was yet the hope of his coming, and the heart of the poet was filled with prophetic visions. Jehovah had sworn, and would not repent. The new high priest was to be forever after the order of Melchizedek, and Jehovah, at his right hand, would strike through kings in the day of his wrath. With the high praises of God in their mouths, and a two-edged sword in their hands, the saints would execute vengeance upon the heathen and punishment upon the nations. And, though few details have survived, it would seem as if the international policy of Simon, without violent struggles, was singularly successful. Even before his formal recognition by the people as the head of a dynasty, he had followed the custom of his brothers and sent again the former ambassador of Jonathan, Numenius, to Rome. There, thanks partly to the present of a golden shield worth 1000 minas, he obtained a renewal of the treaty already made with Judas and Jonathan, in which Rome guaranteed the rights of the Jews and gave to Simon jurisdiction over all Jews, both within and without Judea. The Senate also sent letters to various states and cities, warning them not to trouble Jerusalem. The same embassy also made a treaty with Sparta.

Once only was the peace of Simon's reign seriously endangered. Almost at the time Rome was thus becoming the Jews' confidante, if not champion, Demetrius II, with whom Simon had maintained the best possible understanding, engaged in a campaign with the Parthians, and was captured by their king, Mithridates I (139-138 B.C.). Trypho was accordingly left in undisputed possession of the kingdom. But only for a few days. Antiochus (VII) Sidetes, the brother of Demetrius II, immediately began preparations for seizing the throne. In need of all possible help, he wrote Simon, promising him the right to coin money, freedom from tribute, release from all debts to the crown, and the confirmation of all other rights and privileges. Simon was won over without difficulty, and waited for the opportunity to furnish his new master aid. The opportunity came when, after having defeated Trypho in Upper Syria, Antiochus besieged him in the fortress of Dora, on the coast. Simon then sent Antiochus a force of two thousand men and considerable treasure and arms, but success had made the king less friendly, and he refused to accept the aid, repudiated all his agreements, and sent one of his friends, Athenobius, to force Simon either to surrender Joppa, Gazara, the citadel of Jerusalem, and all the conquered territory outside of Judea, or to pay the enormous sum of 1000 talents. Simon refused to surrender the cities or territory on the ground that they had all either formerly belonged to his people or had done him much injury, but at the same time offered to compromise by the payment of 100 talents. Whereupon, Athenobius, overcome with the luxury of the appointments of the high priest's house, returned to Antiochus in a rage. The king determined to punish such independence. He himself pursued Trypho north through Ptolemais and Orthosias, to Apamsea, where he besieged and killed him, but in the meantime he sent his general, Kendebaus, south against Simon. Jamnia and the neighbouring town of Kedron became the centre of Syrian incursions into Judea. John Hyrcanus, the son of Simon, was in charge of the troops at Gazara, and by the advice of Simon he and his brother Judas moved upon the invaders. The extent to which the military spirit of the Asmoneans had led to a reorganisation of their army is to be seen in the fact that now, for the first time, they employ a small force of cavalry. Jewish generalship and enthusiasm carried the day, and for the remainder of his reign Simon was not troubled by foreign invasion.

And yet Simon, like his four brothers, was to die by violence. A son-in-law, Ptolemy, became ambitious to usurp Simon's place in the nation, and plotted to kill him. His opportunity came when in February, 135 B.C., the high priest came on a tour of inspection to the little fortress of Dok, which was in charge of Ptolemy. There, at a banquet, Simon and two of his sons, Mattathias and Judas, were treacherously killed, and his wife was taken prisoner. Ptolemy also made every effort to seize Hyrcanus, but without success, and this failure, notwithstanding his loyal messages to Antiochus VII, completely prevented his succeeding his victim. Hyrcanus it was who inherited the high-priesthood, and with it the military and civil leadership of the Jews.

Thus a little more than forty years after the first uprising of Mattathias, the last and, unless we mistake, the greatest of his five sons was carried to the tomb he had himself built, having seen his family maintain a successful revolt against a great empire, his people grow from the narrow limits of a city-state into a miniature nation, the high-priesthood together with the supreme military and civil power made hereditary among his own descendants, and Jerusalem and Judea possessed of religious and nearly complete political liberty.

CHAPTER VI: JOHN HYRCANUS AND POLITICAL INDEPENDENCE (135-105 B.C.)

THE tragedy which brought John Hyrcanus to the high-priesthood was prolonged during the first months of his reign. For when he attempted to besiege Ptolemy in Dok, near Jericho, he was repeatedly hindered in his attack by the sight of his mother being tortured on the walls of the fortress. The siege dragged along until a sabbatical year, when it was abandoned, and Ptolemy escaped after having murdered his heroic prisoner.

Other difficulties came upon the State. Antiochus VII, who, after the severe defeat administered by John and Judas to Kendebaus, had allowed the Jews to remain in peace, now took advantage of the death of Simon and invaded Judea in the first year of Hyrcanus. One of the last of strong Syrian monarchs, his forces were more than a match for those of the Jews, and he soon shut John up in Jerusalem and besieged him vigorously. The city was surrounded with a Jerusalem. trench and earthworks, and on its north side were erected a hundred towers three stories in height. Then followed a time, certainly a year in length, in which the Jews within the walls were reduced to the last extremities. The men useless for war were forced to leave the city, but, since Antiochus would not receive them, wandered between the lines, dying miserably of hunger, until the defenders, at the Feast of Tabernacles, readmitted the wretched survivors. But just as Antiochus was about to reduce the city, he raised the siege upon the conditions that the Jews should deliver up their arms, pay tribute for Joppa and the other cities which they had gained, give hostages, break down the city walls, and pay 500 talents of silver (three hundred down) in lieu of admitting a new Syrian garrison into the city.

This sudden leniency on the part of an ambitious king who had victory almost within his grasp was undoubtedly due to some interference of Rome rather than to the fact that he was "religious to the Deity," as Josephus piously remarks. We have thus a victory of the Maccabean policy rather than of Maccabean arms. In fact, the brilliant career of Antiochus demonstrated that the only hope of the Jews' maintaining the position reached by Simon lay either in disturbed Syrian politics or in Roman interference. The little state was too weak to withstand by itself the full strength of Syria. From this time forward dependence upon Rome as an ally and superior becomes increasingly prominent as a feature in the traditional policy of the Asmonean house.

The subsequent relations of Hyrcanus with Antiochus VII were those of friendship. After having thus accepted a vassal's position he supplied his suzerain with military supplies and accompanied him in his expedition against the Parthians. On his part, Antiochus seems to have been considerate of the Jews' religious peculiarities, and on this expedition against the Parthians halted for a couple of days that the Jews need not be forced to march upon Pentecost and the Sabbath.

But Hyrcanus was freed from the strong hand of Antiochus VII by the defeat and death of that monarch among the Parthians, between whom and the Romans Syria was so surely being ground to powder, and in Demetrius II, who was now reinstated on his throne by his captors, Hyrcanus saw if not a friend at least a satisfactorily weak ruler. The inefficiency of Syria was increased, also, by the war between Demetrius II and Alexander Zabinas. Under these favouring circumstances John took up the development of Judea at the point where it had been checked by Antiochus VII, and throughout his long reign was able almost at will to conquer new territory. Medaba fell after a siege of six months, and the fall of Samega, a town probably near Lake Huleh, with its surrounding region followed. Shechem (Nablus) and its dependencies were reduced, the Samaritan temple on Gerizim destroyed. Idumea was thoroughly conquered, and its inhabitants were forced to submit to circumcision under penalty of expulsion, and some of them were colonised in the three Samaritan toparchies given Judea by Demetrius II. So far from being able to oppose such conquests, Demetrius was himself in desperate straits and at last was killed by Alexander Zabinas, who was quite ready to make any treaty Hyrcanus might propose. Even when after a few years Alexander was defeated (122-121 B.C.) and executed by Antiochus VIII (Grypos), Hyrcanus was not disturbed, for the new king was barely able to maintain himself during the first eight years of his reign, and then was deposed by his half-brother, Antiochus Cyzicenus. The struggle between the two rivals lasted for years, and throughout it all Hyrcanus lived in peace. Indeed, since the death of Antiochus Sidetes, he no longer paid the Syrians the least regard, either as their subject or their friend. Thus secure because of Syria's weakness, he again turned upon the ancient enemy of the Jews, "the foolish people who dwelt at Shechem."

When the Jews returned to Judea from Babylon they found the land occupied by a people, Jewish in stock, but mixed with the older inhabitants of the land and with the colonists who had been brought by the Assyrians from the Mesopotamian cities, — Cutha, Ava, Hamath, and Sepharvaim. For awhile the newcomers mingled with this mixed people, and even the high priest was not averse to seeing the Jewish stock corrupted by intermarriage. Ezra and Nehemiah, however, enforced the separation of the "holy seed" from the mixed race and began the erection of a distinctly Jewish state. The Samaritans, who were the most influential of the old people, at first despised and then opposed the reform. But to no purpose. The new Jerusalem was built, the new citizens were separated, and the seeds of lasting enmity were sown. Throughout the centuries that followed each city did its best to injure the other. Each alike honoured Moses, but neither would yield to the religious supremacy of the other. If the temple was in Jerusalem, the Samaritans obtained from Darius Nothus, and again from Alexander, permission to build another upon their holy Mount Gerizim, over which a descendant of Aaron presided. By 170 B.C. the new temple had become a serious rival to that of Jerusalem, and Jews and Samaritans were involved in fierce disputes concerning the relative importance of their two versions of the Law, and the true place of worship. The very fact that the Samaritans were sectaries rather than heathen doubtless deepened the hatred between the two people, and when the Samaritans sided with Syria, war was unavoidable.

Hyrcanus had already destroyed Shechem and the temple upon Gerizim, and now he appeared before the capital city, Samaria, to punish it for the recent injuries done, at the instigation of Syria, to Idumeans he had established as colonists in the three Samaritan toparchies. Despite the aid of Antiochus, the city fell after a siege of a year, and Hyrcanus raised it to the ground, cut canals through it, and made a lake of its site.

With the fall of its ancient rival, Judea reached its greatest prosperity. Like so many other city-states during the decay of the Syrian Empire, it had become independent, and, thanks to its arms and its alliance with Rome, was growing in influence.

But the reign of John Hyrcanus was to do more for Judaism than to give it political independence. It was under him that the two tendencies in the state already mentioned first crystallised into parties with distinctive names, — Pharisee and Sadducee.

The Pharisees constituted the more efficient of two fraternities that grew out of the Chasidim, the Essenes being the second. Their chief inheritance was the legalism of Ezra and Nehemiah, and their central principle was the avoidance of impurity of all sorts. It was this that gave them their name — the Separated.

Throughout the entire revival of Mosaism under the Asmoneans, under the impulse for purity there had been growing up by the side of the Law a rapidly increasing mass of unwritten but authoritative comments and interpretations, the "ancestral tradition" of Paul and the Mishna of the rabbis. Nothing nobler could be asked than the motive from which this "oral law" sprang, and it was its passion for righteousness through obedience to the oral as well as the written law and for purity through separation from everything defiling that made Pharisaism the great influence it became.

So far as their theological and philosophical opinions are concerned, Josephus, who was one of their number, in his formal comparison of their views with those of the Sadducees, declares that the Pharisees held to the immortality of the soul and the resurrection of the body, at least in the case of the righteous a belief that at times runs close to some form of reincarnation or migration of the soul, and is characteristic of most later Jewish religious faith. He also somewhat too sharply describes their position as to free will as a mean between the determinism of the Essenes and the absolute liberty of the Sadducees. The Pharisees he represents as holding that fate co-operates with man in every act, and again states as their opinion that some things are not dependent upon fate, but upon human will. Of their further belief in angels and spirits, Josephus makes no mention, but it is altogether in keeping with their general teaching and the spirit of later Jewish literature in general.

But such matters are secondary. The indispensable element of Pharisaism is its insistence upon righteousness through obedience to Jehovah's law, and upon the withdrawal from everything that might defile. In personal life it led to isolation from the common people, — 'am har'arets, — to repeated washings of the hands, person, dishes, and utensils. In thought it led to infinite devotion to details and preternaturally refined distinctions and warnings. In religion it led to the formation of a fraternity, a church within a church, composed of "Neighbours" who were exclusively scribes, and who were admitted by the laying on of hands. In politics it led to a determination to make Judea complete in itself — an isolated religious commonwealth, as far as possible removed from the contamination of heathen life. The Pharisees, like the Chasidim, at bottom a religious sect, were forced by circumstances into political struggles. But when once they had become the party of the government they looked with apprehension upon foreign alliances, and desired nothing more than an insularity in which they could train up a true Israel — their own fraternity (Chaberim, Neighbours). They were, in fact, by no means a popular party. At the greatest they probably never numbered more than six thousand, each of whom had joined the fraternity in some formal way. Their great political influence was therefore due to the regard in which they were held by the people, both on account of their recognised religious superiority and knowledge of the Law and also because of their hostility to the aristocratic party of the Sadducees.

The Sadducees were not opposed by the Pharisees because of theological differences, although Josephus artificially distinguishes the two parties on such grounds. The ground of opposition lay in the struggles between the latitudinarian aristocrats and the Chasidim. The Pharisees were by origin a body of religionists forced into politics; the Sadducees, a body of aristocrats opposed to the oral law and the later developments of Judaism. Indifferent to religion except as a profession open to priests, disbelievers in immortality of the soul, believers in absolute free will, the Sadducees had been the party of the opposition while Judea had been struggling for liberty; but now that the Asmoneans looked toward national life on a larger scale, they suddenly found themselves brought into new political importance.

From the days of Mattathias, the Asmonean house had been most successful when supported by the Chasidim and their successors. Hyrcanus, no more than his father, desired to break with so virile a following and had been himself counted a Pharisee, yet he was forced to transfer his friendship to the Sadducees.

The occasion for such a revolution in policy as given by Josephus contains too much of the conventional legendary element to be trustworthy, but none the less it may represent some actual occurrence. He represents Hyrcanus as complacently asking his Pharisaic friends at a banquet to point out to him the most certain road to righteousness. All declare him entirely virtuous until the question reaches one Eleazar. This uncompromising servant of the Law declared that if Hyrcanus really would be righteous, he must lay down the high-priesthood and content himself with the civil government. On being pressed for the reason for such an opinion, he declared that it was known that the mother of Hyrcanus had been a captive in the days of Antiochus Epiphanes the implication being that Hyrcanus was not the legitimate son of Simon. Incensed at the insult, Hyrcanus followed the advice of a Sadducee who wished to involve all his opponents in disfavour, and asked the Pharisees to pronounce judgment upon Eleazar. They declared him deserving only of stripes and imprisonment. Hyrcanus, under the insinuations of the Sadducee Jonathan, believed all Pharisees his enemies, and therefore broke with them.

While this story may preserve for us an evidence of the Pharisees' hatred of a warrior high priest, the real reason for the action of Hyrcanus lies deep in the inner life of Judaism. On the one hand the Pharisees must have been deeply disappointed that what had been a holy war should have produced no "kingdom of the saints" — some thoroughly impossible theocracy administered by scribes. They must also have opposed the policy of international treaties, so repugnant to their separatist spirit. The Sadducees, on the other hand, were in sympathy with a broad international policy and looked with favour upon a government of any high priest whatever. It was, therefore, to be expected that they should have been judged to be more serviceable by so thoroughly statesmanlike a man as Hyrcanus. From this time the Sadducees are the party of monarchical nationalism and the Pharisees that of a self-centred, provincial aristocracy.

The break with the "little Judea" party was marked by an undoing of some of their legislation, but even more by expansion in the life of the state. Judea was probably more prosperous than at any time since the reign of Solomon. It is true that its limits were subsequently to be enlarged; l but at no time was it to be freer from internecine struggles or more truly independent of foreign powers. Almost for the first time in its history, commerce began to be of importance. Now that Joppa was safely a Jewish port, the grain, oil, and salt of Judea were exchanged for the luxuries of Egypt and other foreign countries. Already the wealth of the new family was great, while Rome was everywhere enforcing respect for the scattered subjects of its confederate state. Constitutionally, Judea progressed along the lines ordinarily followed by Oriental states, and had lost much of even the half-aristocratic character which it had possessed under Simon. This appears not alone in the fact that, first of all the later Jewish rulers, John Hyrcanus employed mercenaries; the coins of the period furnish some striking evidence of this constitutional change. Some of these bear the inscription, "John the high priest and the congregation of the Jews," but others are inscribed, "John the high priest, head of the congregation of the Jews" — a change full of suggestion as to his position as head of the Jewish state. These facts, coupled with the transference of his sympathies from the Pharisees to the Sadducees, argue strongly that as national independence had succeeded religious liberty, a monarchy disguised as a theocracy was now displacing the city-state. It is in accordance with this general tendency that the Gerousia grows less prominent. A century later it was still the highest court in certain cases, and the very fact that John felt the need of relying upon something corresponding to a modern party, argues that in his day it was possessed of some legislative functions as well. Yet it is not mentioned in the scanty records of the time, and the inference is unavoidable that the Gerousia lost political importance before the rising monarchy. It is, therefore, probably at this time that there began the more academic era in its life which was to reach such development later in the Sanhedrin. Judea had thus all but become a small Oriental monarchy, none the less absolute because its ruler bore the name and exercised the functions of high priest.

Along with these constitutional and political changes, the reign of John Hyrcanus was marked by other important developments within the inner life of Judaism. The Gerousia attacked mixed marriages, classing heathen women with slaves, and, in order to fix more firmly the religious significance of the history in which they had played so large a part, the rabbis drew up a calendar of feast days, commemorating such events as the taking of Akra and Beth-zur. During this period probably still further steps were taken in the completion of the third group of canonical books, the "Sacred Writings." Already the great rabbis had begun to appear — the Zugoth, or "couples," — and in the time of Hyrcanus lived the second "couple," Joshua ben Perachia and Nitai of Arbela, the former of whom taught "Procure a companion for study, and judge all men according to the favourable side." Jews in Alexandria, dazzled by the success of the new dynasty, began to hope for the end of Syrian and Roman supremacy, and, in the alleged words of the heathen Sibyl, could look forward to the time when the "nation of the mighty God should once again be strong, and become to all people the guide of life;" and when an end should be put to all distress, and "from the rising sun, God should send a king who should make all the earth to cease from cruel war, killing some and making faithful treaties with others." Then would "he who formerly gave the Law to the pious, take the kingdom forever over all men."

But this hope for a triumphant Israel was fiercer in the breasts of the Pharisees of Judea, to whom the Asmonean house seemed less of God. If, according to the seer of Alexandria, the nations, seeing how God loved all men, were to throw away their idols and worship in his temple; to the mind of the unknown Pharisee who, in the name of Enoch, burst out in apocalyptic imagery and personification half inspired, half grotesque, the success of the heathen kingdoms and the dominance of the Sadducees, with their "unrighteousness and sin and blasphemy and violence," their "apostasy and transgression and uncleanness," were to bring a merited punishment from the holy Lord, who would execute vengeance upon heathen and apostates in an eternal judgment. Woe was to be theirs who built houses with sin, who acquired gold and silver, who set at naught the words of the righteous, and transgressed the eternal law. Even on the earth they were to suffer, and in the world to come they would confront the record of their evil deeds and go down into a hell of darkness and flame forever; while the righteous should be raised, pure spirits, the joy of angels, to shine as the stars of heaven.

Still another evidence of a rapidly completing Judaism and of differentiating parties is to be seen in one of the enigmas of Jewish history, the esoteric brotherhood of the Essenes, or, more properly, the Essees. Like the fraternity of the Pharisees, it was a descendant of the Chasidim, whose very name, in fact, it still bore. Its genealogical relations with Pharisaism are thus clear. Neither is the offshoot of the other, but both brotherhoods sprang from the same anti-Hellenistic Judaism which it had been the mission of the persecution of Antiochus Epiphanes to consolidate and energise. The continuity of Jewish development is here unbroken. However much Pharisee and Essene might differ as regards important details, each was profoundly devoted to the Thorah, the Sabbath, and to the maintenance of ceremonial purity. Each fraternity, however, had a different future. The Pharisees were swept out into politics; the Essenes were increasingly removing from politics toward the loneliness of the wilderness and the Dead Sea.

Just when the passion for immaculate purity found its first formally organised expression it is impossible to say, but by the time of Hyrcanus, or at least that of his son Aristobulus, it appears to have been complete. Despising wealth and scholastic virtue, the Essene brothers chose a life of celibacy and communism, of devotion to extravagant laws of purity, agriculture, and meditation. Though by no means shunning towns, they kept themselves from, all contaminating influences, repudiating animal sacrifices and slavery. Many of their monastic communities lived in solitudes like Engedi, while others lived in monasteries in the midst of cities, where all who wore the white robe of the fraternity were always welcome.

Entrance to the order was possible only after a novitiate of three years, and this in turn led to further years of instruction in the mysteries of the faith. So far was the principle of purity carried that even among the brothers themselves a higher grade was defiled by contact with a lower. Industrious, modest, profoundly moral and religious, living temperately that they might practice charity, eating their eucharistic meals in solemnity and under the eyes of one whom they had elected their priest, obedient to their president and council, prophets revered by people and kings alike, working their simple cures by magical formulas, herbs, and sacred stones, the Essenes were the admiration of all classes. If it be true that at one time their numbers nearly equalled those of the Pharisees, the fact shows again the respect with which they were held by their fellow-countrymen for their regard for the Law and the Sabbath, as well as the purity of their life. That they had little influence upon national life, that the Pharisees disliked them, that they objected to bloody sacrifices, that they were shut out from the courts of the temple, does not argue the foreign origin sometimes assigned them. Indeed, although they may possibly have originated in Egypt, and although certain of their rites suggest Persian influences, the Essenes were essentially Jewish. They were, in fact, simply carrying to its inevitable conclusion the programme of the Chasidim, and if their belief in angels and heavenly intermediaries, their mysticism and esoteric teachings, find expression, as some believe, in apocalyptic literature like Enoch, it would be only what would be expected.

Thus, in the days of Hyrcanus, the history of the rise and fall of the Jewish state becomes clearly the history of the rise of the party of the Thorah of the Essenes in their protest against form and defilement, and, above all, of the Pharisees in their struggle against Sadduceeism and monarchy.

CHAPTER VII: THE STRUGGLE OF THE PHARISEES WITH THE ASMONEANS AND SADDUCEES 1 (105-69 B.C.)

JOHN HYRCANUS, by his will, made his widow his successor as the political head of the state, and appointed his eldest son, Aristobulus, to the high-priesthood. The arrangement was not only novel; it was fatal to all parties concerned. Aristobulus was not content to share the state with his mother, but shut her up in prison, where she starved to death. With her he imprisoned three of his brothers, thus in genuine Oriental fashion removing all possible claimants to the throne. Strangely enough, however, probably because of some deep attachment, he did not include in the fate of his family his brother Antigonus, with whom he had long been associated in war, but shared his throne with him. This arrangement resulted in the inevitable conspiracy and death that attend divided despotisms. Aristobulus was led to mistrust Antigonus, and by a trick of his queen and his courtiers became the unwitting cause of his death. He died soon after of a loathsome disease and remorse, having reigned but one year.

The reign of Aristobulus, however, though brief (105-104 B.C.), was by no means unimportant. Josephus speaks of him as a friend of the Greeks, although at the same time he is ready to admit that Aristobulus served his country by extending its boundaries. Like his father, Aristobulus endeavoured to build his state upon a common religion. As Hyrcanus had forced circumcision upon the Idumeans, so Aristobulus forced it upon the Itureans of Northern Galilee, and thus completed the Judaising of that region.

But even more important was the constitutional step taken by Aristobulus. Hitherto the Asmonean rulers had laid no claim to the title or insignia of royalty, but Aristobulus broke with the precedents of his house, and marked his entrance into power by assuming a diadem and doubtless the title of king. There is no evidence or, in fact, probability, that the Gerousia regained any of its prestige during his short reign. On the contrary, it probably lost even more of its administrative functions, and became even more judicial or theologically academic. The Jewish theocratic monarchy, in the third generation of the new high-priestly dynasty, crossed the threshold of an absolutism no longer limited by tradition or inherited institutions.

So brief was the reign of this first king of the Jews that no time was given for the Pharisees to organise any strong opposition against his innovation, but opportunity enough was given during the reign of the third son of Hyrcanus, Alexander Jonathan, or, as the word is in Greek, Jannaeus (104-78 B.C.). He, with his brothers, had been imprisoned by Aristobulus, but had been released, married, and raised to the throne by his brother's widow, Queen Salome or Alexandra. The high-priesthood was his, also, by virtue of his kingship, and his abuse of this office, coupled with hatred of the monarchy and its aims, was sufficient to arouse all Pharisees to desperate opposition. A war that had begun for the preservation of the Jewish religion had called to the leadership of the state a family which, after accomplishing religious liberty, had relegated the ancient Gerousia together with the scribes to political insignificance, and turned toward international alliances, foreign conquests, monarchy, and all but declared imperialism. Three toparchies of Samaria, Gazara, and Joppa, as well as other cities, had been added to Judea by Jonathan and Simon, but the ambition of the family of Hyrcanus had been farther reaching. Medaba and Samega, with other cities to the east of Jordan, Shechem, Samaria, Idumea, Bethshean, and Lower Galilee had been conquered and in part made Jewish by the father, and now with the conquest of Upper Galilee by Aristobulus, the ambition of the Asmonean house to found a great kingdom was brought into sharpest contrast with the Pharisees' policy of exclusion and separation.

Alexander set about completing the conquests of his father and brother with all the strength of a reckless nature. With the highlands on the west of Jordan from Lebanon to the desert already his, he turned upon the cities and petty kingdoms to the east of Jordan, and upon the cities of the coast, Ptolemais, Gaza, Strato's Tower, and Dora. While Antiochus Cyzicenus was engaged with Antiochus Philometor, Alexander attacked Ptolemais, beat back its army, and besieged the city. He was not able to take it, however, because of the coming of Ptolemy Lathyrus from Cyprus. Unable to cope with so formidable an antagonist, Alexander raised the siege and tried treachery. Making a treaty with Ptolemy, he also summoned Cleopatra, the mother of Ptolemy, who had but recently driven her son out from Egypt. Ptolemy learned of his ally's unfaithfulness, and immediately marched with most of his force to conquer Judea. He captured and sacked

Asochis in Galilee on a Sabbath, attacked Sepphoris unsuccessfully, and then advanced against Alexander. The battle was fought at Asophon, an unidentified spot on the eastern side of the Jordan valley, and, thanks to Alexander's lack of generalship, the tactics of Ptolemy's general, Philostephanus, and the discipline of his mercenaries, resuited in a complete defeat for the Jews. Thereupon Ptolemy took Ptolemais, which, like Alexander, had proved untrue to him, and ravaged Judea; according to Josephus, boiling and eating women and children. In the meantime Cleopatra had come up from Egypt in pursuit of her son, and proceeded to besiege Ptolemais. Ptolemy, seizing this opportunity, invaded Egypt, but only to be defeated. Thus, by a strange turn of fortune Judea was again about to be subject to Egypt. In fact, nothing prevented such a misfortune except the advice of Ananias, one of Cleopatra's generals, himself a Jew, who foretold a revolt of the Egyptian Jews if such a step were taken. Cleopatra, therefore, renewed her treaty with Alexander, and returned to Egypt.

Alexander was thus left once more free to pursue his policy of expansion. He took Gadara after a siege of ten months, and Amathus, but having lost his baggage and a large number of his men in a sudden attack by Zeno, the local sovereign, he crossed again to the coast. There he captured and sacked Raphia and Anthedon. Gaza was betrayed into his hands after a year's siege, and was plundered and burned, its Council of Five Hundred perishing in the burning temple of Apollo (96 B.C.). He then made a fresh attack upon the region east of Jordan, and succeeded in overcoming the cities and tribes in Moab and Gilead. Amathus, which had revolted, he again took and utterly destroyed. The campaign ended in misfortune, however, as the Arabian Obedas, whose kingdom, or, at least, suzerainty, embraced much of the region between Petra and Hermon, drew the Jews into a narrow ravine near Gadara, and then drove troops of camels down upon them, completely destroying the army. Barely escaping with his life, Alexander fled to Jerusalem, only to find his people in open rebellion.

The explanation of this first revolt against the Maccabean house is not difficult to discover. Alexander had already drawn down upon himself the hatred of the Pharisees and their sympathisers by his disregard of his priestly office. On one occasion, as he had been officiating at the altar during the Feast of Tabernacles, the crowds of worshippers had pelted him with citrons they had brought to the temple, shouting insults to his mother. As a punishment, he had sent his mercenaries against the crowd, and six thousand of the Jews had been killed. Thereafter, Alexander had officiated behind a wooden fence he had built within the Court of the Priests.

Such a punishment of orthodox Jews, the first on the part of any Asmonean, was, in itself, enough to excite the stricter classes, who had already been embittered by the reorganisation of the Gerousia, which, since the last years of Hyrcanus, had been composed wholly of Sadducees, unless we make an exception of the redoubtable Simon ben Shetach, brother of the queen. But more potent than all must have been the deep-seated opposition of the Pharisees to the undisguised usurpations of the high priest. The scandalous stories told of him by Josephus must be in some degree charged to the historian's bias, but the hatred of the Pharisees was intense, and when, after eight years of endurance, it once seemed possible to crush the fugitive king and restore the old constitution, they and their followers rose as a man.

For six years the religious and civil war raged, and fifty thousand Jews are said to have fallen. Then, with one of the untactful attempts at compromise which are to be seen throughout his life, even in the midst of Pharisaic libels, Alexander attempted to treat with his subjects. But their only condition of submission was that he should kill himself, and in a rage of hate they turned for aid to the Syrian king, Demetrius Eucaerus. Such a course was desperate but characteristic of the Pharisees, who now, as later, preferred a foreign ruler and a Gerousia which they might control, to independence and an irresponsible monarch. Demetrius came to the aid of the rebels with a large army, in which were many Jews. Alexander, also with an army of mercenaries and Jews, met him near Shechem. For a while each army endeavoured to cause the defection of their kinsmen from the ranks of the other, but to no purpose, and a battle was finally fought in which Alexander was utterly and hopelessly beaten. Judea was again at the mercy of the Syrians, while the Arabians were kept from invasion only by Alexander's ceding them his conquests in Moab and Gilead.

But the very misfortune of Alexander was to prove his salvation. Six thousand of the Jews who had fought under Demetrius, seeing the dangers to which their land had been exposed by their victory, suddenly deserted Demetrius and joined themselves to their wretched king. Immediately the entire scene changed. Demetrius retired. Alexander, with his new army, repeatedly defeated the rebels, and at last shut up their leaders in the unidentified town of Bethome. The city fell into his hands, and he crucified eight hundred of his prisoners at Jerusalem, after having had their wives and children massacred before their eyes. With this fearful vengeance the civil war came to an end. Eight thousand of the rebels fled from the land, and for the rest of his reign Alexander — known now as the Thracian — kept the peace from his castles of Alexandrium and Machaerus with equal severity and success.

Freed from the opposition of the Pharisees, Alexander could again take up the extension of his kingdom. For a moment, it is true, it seemed possible that the dying Syrian Empire might be revitalised by the energetic Antiochus Dionysius, who would not be kept back by Alexander's ditch and wooden wall across the plain from Antipatris; but Antiochus was defeated and killed by Aretas, king of Arabia, who then came into possession of Ccele-Syria and Damascus. Again the fortunes of Alexander looked dark, for Aretas defeated him at Adida. But the two kings arranged some sort of conditions of peace, and Alexander was again unhampered for foreign war. In this he was brilliantly successful. Within three years Dium, Essa, with the treasures of Alexander's old enemy Zeno, Gaulana, and Gamala, cities on the east of Jordan, together with Seleucia near Lake Huleh, fell into his hands, and doubtless, in accordance with his general relentless policy, were forced to conform to Jewish practices. He returned to Jerusalem, where he was received with great rejoicings. And with reason, for at last the ambition of his house and the pride of the un-Pharisaic portion of his people were in some way satisfied. Thanks to the indomitable warrior, careless as high priest though he may have been, the boundaries of Judea were now approximately those of the best days of David. From the desert to the sea, and from Lebanon to the River of Egypt, there were but few cities which had not accepted Jewish sovereignty and Jewish rites, or, like Pella, been laid in ruins because of their refusal to yield such obedience. Even Damascus seems to have been a subject, or at least under the protection of Alexander. Ascalon on the plain, Ragaba and Philadelphia, on the east of Jordan, alone maintained their independence, and Ragaba fell just as Alexander died.

Yet it would be a mistake to think of the new kingdom as unified. Despite the strenuous efforts of the king, it is clear that the land remained broken up into little regions centring about cities, and also that the heathen were still in the land. These subject cities it was, undoubtedly, that paid the taxes which supported the Jewish state, but they were also liable at any time to fall into the hands of some princeling, like Zeno, and then throw off the Jewish yoke, perhaps, indeed, to rise into actual rivalry with Judea. In fact, they never were thoroughly assimilated, and remained to the end centres of deepening anti-Semitism in the midst of the Jewish territory.

After a reign of twenty-seven years Alexander died, worn out by hardship and dissipation. But he died as he had lived, a warrior. Through these years of failing health he carried on his wars, and at last was overcome by death at the siege of Ragaba, though telling his wife to conceal the fact until the city had fallen.

Alexander's death was to work important changes in Judea. He had never been a friend of the Greeks, and his very wars had been in part for religion. His struggle with the Pharisees had grown from political, rather than religious causes, and it is not improbable that his last years had been marked by something like attempts at reconciliation. At all events, when he found death upon him, he advised Alexandra, who was to succeed him, to depend upon the Pharisees once more. That he was not altogether abandoned by the party of the Law appears in almost the only literary survival of Sadduceeism, the book of 1 Maccabees the work of some sincere but unknown friend of the Asmonean family. Pull of devotion to the Law and of hatred of the Hellenising priests and people of the early days, the book breathes the spirit of un-Pharisaic Judaism. Silent as to the oral law, and deeply religious though it is, it never mentions the name of God. It is something more than the work of a pamphleteer, and in its simple, direct style it tells how the deliverance from Syria resulted, not from the miraculous interposition of Jehovah or the patriotism of the Jews as a people, but from the work of the Maccabees, by whose hand alone was deliverance given unto Israel.

But it was Pharisaism that most found expression during Alexander's reign. Without venturing upon unqualified statements, it may have been at this time that another unknown writer epitomised such portions of an historical work of Jason of Gyrene as told of the early days of the Maccabean house, entitling it the second book of Maccabees. In many particulars it retells more elaborately the story of 1 Maccabees, but its divergences are sufficient to prove its independence of that work. It is, in fact, a Pharisaic reply to 1 Maccabees, avowedly written to show "the manifestation made from heaven in behalf of those who were zealous to believe manfully in defence of Judaism." So full is it of legendary material introduced with this motive, that its chief value (outside its account of certain of the doings of Antiochus IV) lies in its expression of the interpretation put by the Pharisees upon history.

A much more important element of the Pharisaic spirit is seen in those portions of the Book of Enoch which may be with safety referred to the reign of Alexander. The oppressions of Alexander called for vengeance from heaven, and for the establishment of the Messianic kingdom. This latter hope was, it is true, nothing new. It is hard to find a period in the history of the Jews when the more trustful hearts had not been sustained by hope of the coming of some specially empowered person who should cause righteousness and justice to go hand in hand with Jewish victories. But now the misery of those who made God's law their especial delight intensified faith and imagination. They had hoped that the Messiah would appear in some member of the Maccabean house in Judas or John Hyrcanus. But they had been bitterly disappointed. The "kingdom of the saints," which had risen triumphant over the ruins of Syria, had turned out to be but another vulgar monarchy, and the royal high priest only a very earthly ruler, more interested in foreign alliances and in conquered cities than in the Law. And at last a Maccabee had turned his arms against the righteous! With one accord Pharisaism looked to its Bible for encouragement. In the house of David there was some hope, but in the visions of Daniel more. The Son of Man, whom the prophet saw, would certainly once more be seen. He would come to judge the world, to champion and avenge the oppressed, to bring to life all those in Sheol, and give the righteous the earth for an inheritance. A new kingdom would be founded in the place of the Maccabean, composed exclusively of the righteous, forever prosperous and resplendent because of the immediate presence of the Lord of Spirits, Jehovah Himself.

It was this intense Pharisaism, as full of revenge as of faith, that came into power in the person of Alexander's widow, Alexandra (78-69 B.C.). She must have been no ordinary woman who now, after having made her husband king and high priest, established her son Hyrcanus in the high-priesthood, reversed the family policy, and abandoned the Sadducees. Josephus himself, misogynist though he is, pauses to admit that notwithstanding all her faults "she showed no sign of the weakness of her sex," and that "she preserved the nation in peace." In large measure, probably, this success was due to her reliance upon the Pharisees, who had great influence over the people. But, notwithstanding the increased power of the Gerousia, Alexandra was no puppet, and was, as she appears on her coins, a queen.

Secure in the favour of this energetic ruler, the Pharisees began at once the reorganisation of the state. First of all they released those of their number who had been imprisoned, and recalled those who had been banished. But their desire for revenge did not allow them to stop at such beginnings. There began a systematic assassination of Sadducean leaders, which especially sought to cut off the officers of Alexandra, who had had a share in the crucifixion of the eight hundred. So extensive did this mafia become that the old generals of Alexander requested Alexandra to allow them to leave Jerusalem and find safety in control of the frontier fortresses — a request that when granted put into the hands of Sadducean sympathisers all the strongholds except Hyrcanium, Machaerus, and Alexandrium. It is doubtful when this request was granted, and whether it was a part of a widespread plot to gain the kingdom for Aristobulus; but it was to prove serviceable when such a plot came to be formed, toward the end of Alexandra's reign. But peace prevailed throughout the nine years of Alexandra's reign thanks to her connection with the Pharisees, and her mercenaries. Unlike those of her husband, however, these troops were used but little except for preserving the peace, for Alexandra was as sagacious in foreign relations as Alexander had been headstrong. Once only does she seem to have undertaken a war. Then she sent her younger son, Aristobulus, who possessed many of his father's characteristics, to aid Damascus in a struggle with a petty tyrant, Ptolemy Mennaeus. The invasion of Tigranes (70-69 B.C.) for a moment threatened real danger, but Alexandra won his friendship by rich presents, and the interference of the Romans soon made her doubly secure.

That, however, which made the reign of Alexandra of most significance, was the new stage in the development of Judaism consequent upon the ascendancy of the Pharisees. To the two classes of which the Gerousia had been composed, hereditary nobles of the Sadducean party and hereditary priests, there now was added or probably more accurately recognised as belonging a third class, that of the rabbis. From this time forth we can trace the judicial influence of rabbinical Pharisaism. As members of a judicial body, the Pharisees sent their old enemies into banishment, and made the oral tradition, which had grown up within the circle of literati, the law of the land. Over this body the young Hyrcanus presided as high priest, but so utterly lacking was he in energy that Simon ben Shetach, the queen's brother, was its real, though unofficial, head. Associated with him in his reforms was Judah ben Tabbai, who had been induced to come to

Jerusalem from Alexandria for this purpose. Under their influence the Gerousia expunged the severe laws of the Sadducees; ordered more care to be given the examination of witnesses; and made divorce more difficult by the provision that the husband must give the wife he put away some portion of his property. Every feast was better celebrated as a potent reminder of the Pharisees' triumph over their opponents, and that of the Wood Gathering in August as a new impulse to matrimony and patriotism. The support of the national worship in the temple was made secure by the levying of the "half-shekel" upon all Jews above the age of twenty, whether in Palestine or the Dispersion, and what was perhaps most important of all, the foundations of later scribism were laid by the establishment of public schools, which a century later were to be universal in Palestine. It was, in truth, a golden age in the eyes of the scribes a time when all things prospered and Jehovah was so propitious that the scribes preserved the grains of wheat, each as large as a kidney, to show later generations how righteousness exalts a nation, and how sin curses the ground.

But the inevitable reaction came. Oppressed and persecuted in their turn, the Sadducees yet held possession of most of the fortresses of the land, and at the first evidence of the old queen's illness, hastened to prepare a revolt that should prevent the permanent ascendancy of the Gerousia. Hyrcanus II was too weak and too subservient to Simon for their purposes, and they turned to his younger brother Aristobulus, whose hostility to the Pharisees was already open. With the death of Alexandra the struggle between the two parties burst forth as fiercely as during the days of Alexander Jannaeus, and under the leadership of the two brothers Judea plunged anew into a civil war that once more established foreign, rule.

CHAPTER VIII: THE ROMAN CONQUEST OF JUDEA

HOWEVER legitimate a successor of his mother the young high priest, Hyrcanus, may have been, it is clear that the sympathies of his troops were with their old commanders, for when he and Aristobulus met in battle at Jericho, many of his soldiers deserted to the enemy, and Hyrcanus himself was forced to flee to Jerusalem. There he gained possession of the temple area and of the citadel in which the wife and children of Aristobulus had been imprisoned by Alexandra. Probably because of these circumstances Aristobulus was not eager to push his advantage, and within three months from the death of their mother the two brothers came to an amicable agreement. The kingdom and high-priesthood were taken by Aristobulus, and the weak Hyrcanus, reduced to a mere private citizen, was left to the enjoyment of his fortune.

And thus affairs might have remained but for the appearance of an extraordinary man, Antipater, an Idumean, whose father had been governor of Idumea under Alexander Jannaeus and Alexandra. For some reason, perhaps from suspicion of Aristobulus II, he attached himself to Hyrcanus, and endeavoured to rouse him into something like self-respect, if not revolt. At first his efforts were unavailing, but at last he persuaded Hyrcanus that his brother threatened his life, and induced him to flee to Aretas, king of Arabia. Once secure in the friendly court at Petra, Antipater found no difficulty in persuading Hyrcanus to ask aid from Aretas against Aristobulus. The king consented, but demanded the return of the territory and the twelve cities Alexander had taken. These terms once granted, Aretas, Antipater, and Hyrcanus, at the head of fifty thousand men, marched against Aristobulus, defeated him, and drove him into the temple and citadel of Jerusalem. There they besieged him, Jerusalem itself being divided, the people favouring Hyrcanus, but the priests, Aristobulus. The struggle was carried on with great bitterness the first war for succession in the history of the Maccabean house. The principal Jews deserted the city and went to Egypt; but neither party would yield. Cruelty and bad faith increased the madness, while a furious storm due, as the priests believed, to the impiety of the besiegers brought a famine upon the entire land.

Doubtless, sooner or later, Aristobulus must have yielded, if only from hunger; but before such an extremity was reached a new factor appeared in Jewish politics. For years the Romans had been closing in upon the Syrian and neighbouring kingdoms, and at last the desperate struggles of Tigranes had led to the expedition of Pompey. Armed with unprecedented powers, Pompey had succeeded in reducing Asia to something like order, and in 65 B.C. sent his general, Scaurus, to secure Syria. Scaurus arrived at Damascus only to find himself anticipated by two of Pompey's other generals, Lollius and Metellus. At once he started toward Judea, but before he could reach Jerusalem the two brothers heard of his approach, and, true to the traditional Roman policy of their family, each sent an embassy, promising a present of 400 talents for a favourable decision. Scaurus decided in favour of Aristobulus, as his seemed to be the more promising cause, ordered Aretas to return to Arabia, and himself returned to Damascus. Thereupon Aristobulus attacked the besieging force, and completely defeated it.

Neither party regarded the quarrel settled, however, for when Pompey himself arrived in Syria, in the winter of 64-63 B.C., Aristobulus sent him ambassadors, and a wonderful golden vine worth 500 talents, and a little later other ambassadors came from Hyrcanus and Antipater. Postponing all decision, Pompey devoted himself to the reduction of the petty states of Coele-Syria, and in the spring arrived in Damascus. There the representatives of the two brothers again met him, and with them those of the Pharisees, who requested that neither brother be recognised as king, but that the state be allowed to enjoy its old government of the high priest and Gerousia.

The latter request Pompey seems to have ignored, and after condemning the violent proceedings of Aristobulus and ordering both brothers to keep the peace, he deferred his decision until he had made an expedition against the Nabateans and had then come into of Judea. He then set out upon his campaign, probably taking Aristobulus and Hyrcanus with him. When they arrived at Dium, however, Aristobulus suddenly fled to the beautiful fortress of Alexandrium, just inside the borders of Judea. There in that castle which was later to contain the bodies of so many of the last unhappy Maccabees, he proposed to stand a siege. He was, however, forced to surrender all his fortresses to the Romans, and retired in a rage to Jerusalem to prepare for war.

Hearing of this revolution Pompey marched down to Jericho, then luxuriant with palms and balsams, and, after a single night's rest, went up to Jerusalem. Again Aristobulus weakened, came out to meet Pompey, and promised to pay over a large sum of money and to surrender the city if only the Romans would leave the country in peace. With his customary willingness to avoid unnecessary injury to a dependent people, Pompey agreed to the proposals, and sent Gabinius to receive the money and the city. But when that general appeared at the gates of Jerusalem, he found the sympathies of its inhabitants divided. On the one hand, the great mass of the population was desirous of avoiding bloodshed and of receiving the Romans; but on the other, the soldiers of Aristobulus would listen to no proposition of surrender, closed the gates fast, and sent Gabinius back to Pompey empty-handed. Naturally enraged at this unfaithfulness, Pompey threw Aristobulus into chains, and proceeded against Jerusalem. Within the city, the party of Aristobulus seized the temple, but the other admitted Pompey's army into the city proper. Then there began the siege of the temple, which was by no means successful until, taking advantage of the Jews' unwillingness to engage in offensive operations on the Sabbath, Pompey was able to build a great bank opposite the north wall of the temple, on which to set his artillery. For three months the siege continued, but the wall was broken on the Day of Atonement (October, 63 B.C.), and the Romans rushed into the temple, butchering the priests at the altar. Twelve thousand Jews are said to have fallen. Pompey, with a few of his friends, entered the Holy of Holies; but left all the treasure of the temple, amounting to 2000 talents, untouched. The day after the capture, the worship of the temple began again at his command with Hyrcanus II as high priest. Aristobulus and his family graced Pompey's triumph in Rome, and large numbers of captives were carried to the capital, where they raised the Jewish colony to great importance, even if they may not be said to have founded it.

Thus almost exactly a hundred years from the triumphs of Judas Maccabaeus, and only eighty since its independence was fairly achieved, Judea once more and finally fell into the control of a foreign power. Before leaving the country, Pompey stripped it of most of the territory won since the days of Simon, and made the remainder, with the high priest, subject to his representative in Syria, Scaurus, who was left for two years in charge of the entire region between Egypt and the Euphrates, with full praetorian power.

Just how long Hyrcanus could have maintained this somewhat uncertain position, is a question; but after six years the revolt of Alexander, the son of Aristobulus, led to a thorough reorganisation of the government under Gabinius, who at that time (57 B.C.) was in charge of the Roman affairs in Syria.

Hyrcanus was left in possession of the high-priesthood, but was deprived of all political power, which now, quite after the plans of the Pharisees, was vested in an aristocracy. Judea was divided into five districts, at the head of each of which was the council of its chief city, — Jerusalem, Gadara, Amathus, Jericho, Sepphoris.

These councils were primarily courts (sanhedrins), but in addition to their judicial functions probably had charge of the taxes and local affairs, and were subject to the proconsul of Syria.

The feelings with which a proud people thus saw a national future suddenly disappear, a dynasty removed, and a new master established, appear in part in the bitter comment of Josephus upon the Asmonean house, but even more in the Psalms of the Pharisees' or as they are better known, the Psalms of Solomon. In them appear alike the Pharisees' contempt for the Asmonean house, righteous indignation at its disloyalty to its sacred office, sorrow for the miseries of the nation, and complete assurance that in the death of Pompey God was punishing the instrument of his wrath. Along with the political feeling there ran a passionate moral indignation. Divine punishment awaited the hypocrite and sinner, but justification and help the righteous. In addition, the new conditions so unfavourable to any political career made the study of the Thorah a matter of course. "Love work, hate authority, and do not press thyself upon the great," was the advice of Shemaiah, the successor of Simon ben Shetach, and from this time begins a new succession of great teachers of scribism, who were almost without exception, members of the Pharisaic society.

With this transformation there went of necessity the end of political struggles between the Pharisees and the Sadducees. Neither could now hope for victory over the other and were at one in their hatred of the Romans. Yet each still pursued its own ends, and in the region of religion, at least, their old conflict. The Pharisee grew more intense in his search for righteousness in accordance with the oral law, the Sadducee grew more content to point out the weaknesses of his opponent, to annoy him by subtle questions, and to await stoically the decrees of Providence. To each alike God seemed to grow farther away. If the Sadducee introduced a mediatory Wisdom, the Pharisee saw his God only at the end of an interminable succession of duties, and represented on earth by his word (memra; bath qol). Righteousness became increasingly dependent upon rabbinical learning a possession possible only to the aristocracy of the schools. God himself became a rabbi, read every Sabbath in the Bible, and became entangled in an all-embracing scholasticism.

Yet, through this arid legalism bred of thought that could not deal with politics, there ran a genuinely spiritual hope. Sick at heart of all attempts to found a political kingdom, the faith of Pharisaism looked more eagerly for the coming of King Messiah. The misery of the days that stirred the indignation of the writer of the Psalms of the Pharisees, brought with it also the lesson that God's kingdom must be something other than that of the Asmoneans. From this conviction there burst the splendid vision of a new kingdom of saints:

And a righteous king and taught of God is he that reigneth over them.

And there shall be no iniquity in his days in their midst; for all shall be holy and their king is the Lord Messiah.

For he shall not put his trust in horse and rider and bow; nor shall he multiply unto himself gold and silver for war; nor by ships shall he gather confidence for the day of battle.

The Lord himself is his king, and the hope of him that is strong in the hope of God.

And he shall have mercy upon all nations that come to him in fear.

He himself also is pure from sin, so that he may rule a mighty people, and rebuke princes and overthrow sinners, by the might of his word.

And who can stand up against him?

He is mighty in his works and strong in the fear of God,

Tending the flocks of the Lord with faith and righteousness; and he shall suffer none to faint in their pasture.

Henceforth the Messianic hope in the hearts of many Pharisees grew less political, and in its stead there is to be seen a desperate belief that the new and glorious kingdom must await the triumph of the Law and the resurrection of the dead. That this eschatological hope was not the hope of the people at large, goes without saying. That it could not steady a people under extreme provocation was, unfortunately, also to appear.

CHAPTER IX: THE RISE OF THE HOUSE OF ANTIPATER

DURING the ten years of political decadence that followed the Roman conquest of Judea, the weak Hyrcanus came increasingly under the control of his self-appointed patron, Antipater. The aid he was able to render to Scaurus in bringing Aretas to terms gave Antipater new importance; but even more was obtained from his services during the attempt of Aristobulus II to reinstate himself on the throne, after his escape from Rome in 56 B.C., and, later, when Gabinius, at the command of Pompey, gave up his expedition against the Parthians in order to reinstate Ptolemy Auletes in Egypt, he not only furnished the Roman forces with supplies, weapons, and money, but won over the Jews who controlled the passes leading to Egypt. Afterward, when Alexander, the son of Aristobulus II, had again undertaken to head a revolt against Rome, Antipater was sent by Gabinius to the Jews who favoured the movement, if possible, to prevent the revolt becoming universal. In this Antipater was successful, although he could not win over Alexander himself. In return, he seems to have been put in charge of the finances of Judea, and Gabinius seems to have followed his advice implicitly in dealing with the affairs of Jerusalem. Antipater, in the meantime, also made friends among influential men generally, and especially with the king of Arabia, one of whose relations, Cyprus, he married. Yet, throughout these years he never attempted to remove Hyrcanus from the high-priesthood, and, although dictating his policy, seems to have shown him the utmost respect.

This growing importance of Antipater saved the Jews from the miseries that might have befallen them under the first triumvirate and during the Civil Wars, although Antipater was unable to prevent the avaricious Crassus from plundering the temple in direct violation of his oath not to take more than what was offered him. From this time Syria was in miniature the Roman republic. Most of the great leaders of the struggles begun by Caesar and Pompey at some time were within its limits. And what was true of Syria was almost equally true of Palestine. At first Antipater favoured Pompey, while Aristobulus and his sons were supported by Caesar. But the friends of Pompey succeeded in poisoning

Aristobulus II just as he was departing for Palestine at the head of two legions given him by Caesar, and shortly after the father-in-law of Pompey, getting possession of Alexander, beheaded him at Antioch. After the defeat and death of Pompey, however, Hyrcanus and Antipater immediately changed sides and supported Caesar. Fortunately, they were able to render him decisive aid. At the moment when Caesar's affairs were desperate at Alexandria, Antipater heard that Caesar's ally, Mithridates, was unable to move beyond Askelon because of the enmity of the border tribes, and especially of the city of Pelusium. He immediately took a force of three thousand men and marched to his relief. In a surprising way he became for a moment one of the determining factors in universal history. He won over the Arabs and Syrians from Lebanon to the desert; led the storming party that broke down the wall of Pelusium; by means of letters from the high priest, won over the Jews of Egypt who had been at first hostile to Caesar, so that they not only allowed the passage of the troops, but supplied them with provisions; and, finally, in the decisive battle that gave Caesar control of Egypt, snatched victory out of defeat by coming to the aid of Mithridates just as his forces were being put to flight. When the news of these services reached Caesar, he readily overlooked the past and won Antipater over more completely by the promise of further service and reward. But more important, in gratitude for the services of Antipater, Caesar restored to the Jews many of their privileges which Pompey had destroyed. Instead of favouring Antigonus, the younger son of Aristobulus II, who urged that he be given the kingdom of which he complained Antipater and Hyrcanus had deprived him, Caesar confirmed Hyrcanus as hereditary high priest (possibly he had already appointed him hereditary ethnarch), and made Antipater a Roman citizen and procurator of Judea. It also appears that some of its old judicial rights were returned to the Gerousia. He further granted Hyrcanus the right to rebuild the walls of Jerusalem, abolished the divisions of Gabinius, gave the Jews freedom from supporting Roman soldiers or furnishing auxiliaries, a reduction of their tribute during the sabbatical year, and the possession of Joppa. Subsequently several other places were restored; the Jews were termed the confederates of the Romans; their religious customs were still fully guaranteed them, not alone in Judea, but in Alexandria and elsewhere, and their feasts were excepted from legislation against "Bacchanal rioting," both in Rome itself and in the provinces. The Jews of Alexandria were further recognised as citizens of that place. In the light of these privileges it is little wonder that the Jews should have been among the most sincere mourners of Caesar's death.

Thus established as representative of Rome in Judea, at least coordinate with the high priest, Antipater at once proceeded to build up the fortunes of his family, as well as to restore tranquillity to Judea. His son, Phasaelus, he made governor of Jerusalem and its surrounding country; while Herod, his younger son, he put in charge of Galilee. An opportunity for displaying his energy met Herod at the outset of his administration in Galilee. Ezekias, a captain of a large band of robbers, or quite as likely, rebels, had made himself the scourge of the neighbouring regions of Syria. Herod came upon him, captured him, and executed him together with a number of his followers, to the great delight of the Syrians. Phasaelus, not to be outdone by his brother, devoted himself to the administration of Jerusalem, and in his turn won new honour and popularity for his family, and especially for his father. Herod's prompt punishment of Ezekias, however, met with the disapproval of the Council or Sanhedrin of Jerusalem, which seems to have possessed the exclusive power of life and death in Galilee, as well as in Judea proper, and aided by the demands of the mothers of the men who had been killed, the Sanhedrin persuaded Hyrcanus to order Herod to come to Jerusalem for trial. At the advice of Antipater, the young man came attended by a bodyguard of considerable size. Just how the case might have turned is not certain, for Sextus Caesar, the governor of Syria, wrote Hyrcanus threatening trouble unless Herod was acquitted; and as the sentence of death was about to be pronounced by the court, Hyrcanus adjourned the session until the next day. During the night Herod took the advice of Hyrcanus and fled to Damascus, where he bought from Sextus Caesar the position of general of the army of Coele-Syria, and prepared to make war on Hyrcanus. From this purpose, however, he was deterred by Antipater and Phasaelus, and for several months was apparently engaged in aiding Sextus Caesar in quieting Syria, where the party of Caesar was not yet supreme.

In 46 B.C., however, the friends of Pompey, in that province, gathered about Caecilius Bassus, killed Sextus Caesar and began a civil war, whose outcome finally came to depend upon the siege of Apamaea, where the Pompeians had concentrated (45 B.C.). In this struggle Antipater sent troops to aid the party of Caesar, but no decided advantage had been won by the new governor of the province, L. Statius Murcus, when Caesar himself was assassinated March 15, 44 B.C. In the civil war that followed,

Lucius Cassius went to Syria to raise troops and funds in behalf of the conspirators. No sooner had he arrived than both Murcus and Bassus at Apamaea went over to him. Possessed thus of Syria, Cassius proceeded at once to levy exorbitant taxes upon the unfortunate provincials, Judea's quota being set at 700 talents. Antipater attempted no resistance to the new ruler, but seized the opportunity of proving the serviceableness of his family. He at once set about the collection of this sum, dividing the task among Phasaelus, Herod, and his enemy Malichus. Herod showed so much zeal in collecting the portion that fell to Galilee that Cassius reappointed him general of Coele-Syria, giving him both land forces and a fleet.

The withdrawal of Cassius from Judea was followed by the murder of Antipater. Malichus, apparently one of the numerous Jews who wished a reinstatement of the old theocratic government under Hyrcanus, some time previously had attempted to put Antipater out of the way, but had been detected and forgiven. But when the future of Roman control seemed threatened, Malichus renewed his conspiracy and succeeded in poisoning Antipater as he was dining with Hyrcanus (43 B.C.), and immediately attempted to head a revolt. Thereupon, with the connivance and even encouragement pf Cassius, Herod had him assassinated at Tyre, to the speechless astonishment of Hyrcanus, who now came under the control of Phasaelus and Herod.

The final withdrawal of Cassius from Syria was followed by general disorder. The Roman commandant, Felix, attempted to put Phasaelus under arrest, but was defeated even before Herod could send his brother aid; the party of Malichus, more or less with the support of Hyrcanus, broke into revolt and occupied several castles, chief among which was Masada; Antigonus, son of Aristobulus II., endeavoured to regain Judea for his family, with the aid of Ptolemy, the son of Mennaeus of Chalcis, while Marion, the tyrant of Tyre, not only aided Antigonus, but himself captured three fortresses in Galilee.

But after the defeat of Brutus and Cassius at Philippi (42 B.C.), Antony came to the east to reestablish Roman control. He was met in Bithynia by an embassy from Judea, praying him to remove Phasaelus and Herod and to reinstate Hyrcanus in something more than a semblance of power. Apparently, the case was hopeless for the former allies of Cassius, but Herod purchased the good will of Antony, and the embassy was not even given a hearing. A second deputation asking for the undoing of the acts of

Cassius was, however, more successful, and Antony restored to liberty all those whom Cassius had sold for non-payment of taxes.

On the arrival of Antony in Antioch, a deputation of one hundred prominent Jews met him with new accusations against the sons of Antipater, especially Herod, whose insult to the Sanhedrin was doubtless still a source of hatred. But the remembrance of his former friendship with Antipater, together with the testimony of Hyrcanus himself to the good administration of Herod, led Antony to decide in favour of the accused, and to imprison and later to execute fifteen members of the deputation. He indeed did more, for he appointed Phasaelus and Herod tetrarchs, with full political power, Hyrcanus retaining, therefore, as he had under Pompey, simply the power of the high-priesthood, stripped of all political power. A subsequent embassy of a thousand Jews, which endeavoured to persuade Antony to reverse his decision, was driven back by soldiers, and the state was apparently fixed in the hands of the Idumean family the subjects and appointees of Rome.

CHAPTER X: HEROD I AND THE CHANGE OF DYNASTY (40-4 B.C.)

THE good fortune of Herod was, however, about to suffer an eclipse. The favours which he and Phasaelus received from the Romans had been from the start distasteful to the leading men of the Pharisees, and the treatment accorded their deputations by Antony, as well as the new taxes laid by the luxurious conqueror, had naturally increased their discontent. When, therefore, during Antony's stay with Cleopatra in Egypt (40 B.C.), Antigonus once more attempted to get possession of the throne by the aid of the Parthians, whom he won over by the promise of 1000 talents and 500 women, he found many sympathisers in Judea. The Parthian invasion consisted of two detachments. One under Pacorus, son of the Parthian king, marched along the maritime plain, and the other under the satrap Barzatharnes, through the interior. The first attack of Antigonus was with a small force of Parthian horsemen and Jews from the neighbourhood of Carmel upon the king's palace in Jerusalem, but was unsuccessful. Thereupon he waited in the vicinity of the city, keeping up desultory fighting until Pentecost, hoping that he might then gather recruits from those who came up to attend the feast. In this he was successful, and soon had a large force behind him. Yet he seems to have preferred treachery to fighting. Through his request the commander of the Parthian troops (whose relations with Antigonus were not known to Herod and his brother) was allowed to enter the city and hold a conference with Phasaelus and Hyrcanus. Despite the warning of Herod, he persuaded them to go to the commander of the main body of invaders in Galilee. By him they were treacherously thrown into chains. Shortly after Phasaelus beat his brains out, and Hyrcanus was carried as a captive to Babylon, after his ears had been cut off, that he might never again be high priest. The Parthians then plundered Jerusalem and neighbouring portions of Judea, finally leaving Antigonus to reign as king and high priest (40-37). In the meantime Herod, having been warned by Phasaelus, fled by night with a considerable force, expecting to find asylum at Petra with the Arabian king Malchus, whom he had previously aided. When, however, he started for Petra, he was met by messengers telling him not to proceed farther, as Malchus would not receive him. Thereupon he determined to go to Egypt, and thence to Rome.

Nothing could be more dramatic than the events of the next few weeks. Herod arrived at Pelusium and persuaded the naval officers to take him to Alexandria. Cleopatra heard of his arrival and endeavoured to persuade him to spend the winter with her as commander of an expedition she was fitting out. But not even she and the danger of winter travel could stop him. After a terrible passage he arrived at Rhodes, only to find the city in ruins and no vessel to carry him to Rome. He built (or at least equipped) a three-decked ship, besides restoring the city during his delay. At last he arrived at Brundusium, and travelled post-haste to Rome and Antony. His purpose in thus seeking aid at Rome was to get the young Aristobulus, grandson of Hyrcanus II and brother of Mariamme, appointed king, doubtless that he might repeat the career of Antipater. But when he had made his complaint and given the necessary bribes, Antony and Octavius preferred to appoint Herod himself king, because of his evident capacity to protect the frontier against the Parthians, and persuaded the Senate to act accordingly. The next day, the first of his reign, Herod was feasted by Antony, and within a week after his arrival in Italy was sailing back to Palestine, a king in search of his kingdom (40 B.C.). In the meantime Antigonus had assumed the high-priesthood with the royal title, and the Parthians had been driven from Syria by Ventidius, the legate of Antony, southward into Judea, whither he followed them ostensibly to relieve Joseph (whom his brother Herod had left in charge of his family Masada) from danger from Antigonus. In reality, Ventidius did little except mulct Antigonus of large sums. Accordingly, when Herod arrived at Ptolemais, he found that the entire work of putting down his rival was to be his, and even in this he was handicapped by the fact that Silo, the lieutenant of the legate, was soon afterward bribed into inactivity by Antigonus. Yet he began the work of conquering his country. The Galileans joined him in considerable numbers, and what with them and other Jewish forces, as well as Roman and mercenary troops, he was soon in a position to march south. Joppa was seized and garrisoned, his friends in Masada were at last relieved from the peril of their position, the fortress of Thresa was captured, and then Herod moved upon Jerusalem. Here Silo made it impossible for him to enter vigorously upon a siege, and, despite his utmost efforts, Herod was unable to prevent the Roman forces from going into winter quarters. Thereupon, in an exceptionally severe winter, he sent his brother Joseph to conquer

Idumea, while he himself recovered Galilee. Samaria seems to have offered no resistance to his claims, for he left his family within it. In Galilee he found his chief opponents in the robbers who inhabited the caves at Arbela, near the Sea of Galilee. At first Herod was unable to subdue them, but later let his soldiers down in great boxes and baskets from the top of the cliffs, and so destroyed them in their very caves. As a punishment for their defection he also laid upon the cities a fine of 100 talents. A little later, after the defeat of the Parthians by Ventidius, Antony ordered Machaeras with a considerable force to go to the aid of Herod. Again, however, Antigonus succeeded in bribing the Roman commander, but prevented his entering Jerusalem. Herod none the less visited Antony, who received him with great honour, and after the surrender of Samosta, gave him two legions.

This visit of Herod to Antony, however, nearly cost him his kingdom. For during his absence Joseph allowed himself to be surprised during harvest at Jericho, and together with a large portion of his troops was killed. This defeat was the signal for widespread revolt against Herod. Galilee rose and drowned his officers in the lake, and a large part of Judea also became seditious. Herod received news of these misfortunes while in Daphne, near Antioch, and marched at once against Antigonus at the head of a legion and eight hundred auxiliaries. His first attack upon Galilee was not successful; but upon the arrival of a second legion from Antony he was able to march upon Jericho. There he hospitably received the principal men of the country and beat back an attack of the enemy, and shortly afterward defeated Pappus, a general of Antigonus. After this success, all Judea, with the exception of Jerusalem, fell into his hands, and as soon as spring came he began the siege of the capital, three years after he had been appointed king. So assured did his success now seem, that in the midst of the siege he was married to Mariamme, the daughter of Alexander, the son of Aristobulus II, and on her mother's side the granddaughter of Hyrcanus II one of the most beautiful women of her day, and to whom Herod had been for several years betrothed.

Shortly after his marriage, Herod was reenforced before Jerusalem by Sossius and the main army of Antony. With eleven legions of infantry, six thousand horse, and a considerable force of auxiliaries, it was only a question of time before Jerusalem should fall into his hands. Yet the forces of Antigonus fought desperately, and it was not until five months after the beginning of preparations that Antigonus yielded, threw himself on his face at the feet of Sossius and begged for mercy. The Roman insulted him, called him "Antigone," and threw him into chains. In the meantime the Roman soldiers pillaged the city, slaughtering all whom they met, until Herod succeeded in saving the inhabitants from utter destruction by promising his allies enormous rewards. When Sossius left, he carried with him Antigonus as a prisoner, intending to take him to Antony, who in turn proposed to take him to Rome to grace his triumph. But Herod feared the result of allowing him to go to Rome, and by a large gift persuaded Antony to have him beheaded, according to Strabo it being the first instance in which the Romans had executed such a sentence upon a king. Although the Asmonean family still existed in the persons of Hyrcanus II, his daughter, and grandchildren, Herod had now no rival claimant for the throne. The Asmonean dynasty was at an end, and their "Mayors of the Palace" were installed as their political successors.

It was no ordinary man that thus came to the Judean throne, at last forever separated from the high-priesthood. For if Herod is at times the "splendid Arab" of Renan, the slave of conspirators in his women's quarters, he is at others the astute ruler able to keep in check a headstrong people and maintain the friendship of Augustus, a builder of cities, a Roman man of the world, and the indispensable guardian of the Arabian frontier. As king, he was one of a large number of semi-dependent "allied kings" (reges socu), who might not even use the royal title without the consent of Rome. Their powers varied considerably, but in general were only sufficient to enable them to be inexpensively serviceable to the Empire. Their rights were not always, if commonly, based upon treaties, and thus both within and without the Empire their position was in some respects not unlike that of the mediaeval vassal. They were not always obliged to pay tribute, but were expected to furnish military aid whenever it was needed. Gifts were also expected. Allied kings had the right of coining money — in Herod's case restricted to copper. Military power was likewise given them, but a too elaborate military establishment was liable to cause suspicion. In fact, the entire relation of these kings to the Empire was not unlike that of the German princes to Napoleon I. If the "allied king" kept order within his territory and on the frontier, he was shown plenty of respect; but if he proved inefficient, he was pretty sure to be deposed, even if his territory was not made a part of a province.

The reign of Herod is of less historical than biographical interest. After he had once gained undisputed possession of Judea, there could be little constitutional change, and even the disproportionate importance sometimes given a country by a desperate war was denied Judea. Yet so astute a ruler as he proved to be, could not fail to leave some impression upon the state. In the management of the foreign relations of Judea he barely missed greatness. Thrust in between uneasy border chiefs and the Roman Empire, a king over a people that, except for brief intervals, always hated him, he was yet so consummate an opportunist as to win and hold the favour of successive rivals. In fact, the only enemy whom he failed either to placate or to worst was Cleopatra of Egypt, especially dangerous because of her influence over Antony and her determination to get possession of the palm groves of Jericho as well as the surrounding region of the Jordan valley. His reign was of national significance also, not only because of the increased size of his kingdom, but also because of the rapid increase of Hellenism in the country. Unlike that of the days of Antiochus IV, however, this later Hellenism seems to have affected Jewish religious life but little within Palestine itself. Heathen cities grew more prosperous and the heathen population of the land increased. Jerusalem itself had its theatre, amphitheatre, and games. The more pious Jews held themselves aloof from these surroundings, but none the less the new factors were to prove of considerable importance in political affairs, and if we may judge by the events of 66 A.D. the increased hatred of the Gentile was accompanied by an equally strong hatred of the Jew.

But doubtless most important of all the national results of Herod's reign was the consolidation of Pharisaism. At the outset, the Pharisees seeing in him the enemy of Antigonus and Sadducaism had favoured Herod, and their two leaders, Pollio — possibly the celebrated Abtalion — and his pupil, Shemaia, had advised Jerusalem to open its gates to him. Herod's wholesale massacre of the Sadducean aristocracy and his reorganisation of the Sanhedrin under Pharisaic influence, confirm this opinion. It was under Herod, also, that the two best-known Jewish rabbis taught, — Shammai and Hillel. Of these two really great men, Shammai is represented as the sterner and more uncompromising; Hillel the gentler and more liberal. Yet this difference was rather with the refinements of the Law. As regards its ethical content they were at one. Shammai bade his disciples "make the study of the Law a decided occupation, promise little and do much, and receive every one with kindness;" while no Jewish teacher has left so many profound ethical sayings as Hillel. "Do not to others what thou wouldst not have done to thyself. This is the principal commandment; all others are the development of that one." "He who wishes to raise his name, lowers it; he who does not seek the Law, does not deserve to live. He who does not progress in learning retrogrades; he who uses the crown of the Law for his own ends, perishes" — these are but two of his sayings. Under Hillel, also, the confused exegetical method of the earlier scribes was systematised and reduced to seven rules; while his practical sagacity appeared when, as president of the Sanhedrin, he procured the passage of a law regulating the cancellation of debts in the sabbatical year, which was proving injurious to business enterprise.

The reign of Herod not only saw both Pharisees and Sadducees withdraw from political life; it saw the latter utterly stripped of political significance. Obscure men from Babylon and Alexandria were elevated to the high-priesthood, and the office itself came wholly within the control of the new king. At the very beginning of his reign, Herod broke the power of the old Sadducean aristocracy by executing forty-five of its most wealthy members and confiscating their property, and as a result throughout his life he was free from any danger from that quarter.

But beyond these limits the reign of Herod has small historical significance, and its interest lies in those personal affairs so minutely copied by Josephus from the king's historiographer, Nicholas of Damascus.

Safe from any serious opposition from the nation, Herod was rich in rivals in the members of the Asmonean house, Hyrcanus II, his daughter Alexandra, and her children Aristobulus and Mariamme, his own wife. The first attitude of Herod toward these members of his family was altogether friendly. He had always been on good terms with the old Hyrcanus, and at the beginning of his reign induced him to return from Babylon. On his arrival in Jerusalem, Herod received him with distinction, gave him the most honourable seat at banquets, called him father, and in every way possible endeavoured to replace him in his old position. High priest, Hyrcanus could not be because of the loss of his ears, and Herod accordingly appointed his friend Ananel, an obscure Jew from Babylon, to the office. Herod's mother-in-law, Alexandra, however, a scheming, selfish woman, took it ill that her son Aristobulus should not have been chosen to succeed his grandfather and uncle, and immediately began to intrigue with Cleopatra in hopes of Antony's support. The means she chose to bring her ends to pass were worthy of the age, the woman, and the man, but proved ineffectual. Herod, nevertheless, judged it politic to reinstate the Asmonean family in the high-priesthood, and after deposing Ananel, appointed Aristobulus.

But although apparently reconciled, Herod and Alexandra were really struggling for the control of the state. Herod's suspicions, aroused by a knowledge of this fact, were deepened by Alexandra's attempt to escape with Aristobulus to Cleopatra, his implacable enemy, and after he saw the enthusiasm aroused by the bearing and beauty of Aristobulus as he officiated at the Feast of Tabernacles, he judged it no longer safe to allow the boy to live. Shortly after the feast, Aristobulus was drowned, apparently accidentally, while he was bathing in one of the fish ponds of his mother's palace at Jericho, and Ananel once more became high priest. Alexandra never doubted Herod's complicity in her son's death, and succeeded in having the king brought to trial before Antony, who just then came to Laodicea on the Syrian coast. Herod went with trepidation, leaving his uncle, Joseph, in charge of the state and the royal household, with orders to kill Mariamme in case he should not return. This genuinely barbarian foresight was to bring Herod even more deeply into trouble with his wife and mother-in-law. On his return, his sister Salome, who was madly jealous of the Asinonean women, accused Mariamme of unfaithfulness. His suspicion was strengthened by Mariamme's reference to his secret orders to Joseph, and in a rage of jealousy he executed Joseph, put Alexandra under guard, and all but killed Mariamme.

During the latter part of the supremacy of Antony and Cleopatra, Herod was forced to pay rental, not only for Jericho, but also for Arabia, a fact that plunged him at one time into the greatest danger. The Arabian king refused to pay the proper tribute, and Herod undertook to enforce his demands, but was utterly defeated, and for some time was unable to gather any considerable army or carry on anything beyond guerila war. It was not for several months, indeed until after the battle of Actium, that he was able to bring the Arabians again into subjection.

The victory of Octavius at Actium might easily have ended Herod's career. He had been the friend of Antony, and indeed had been prevented from sending him troops only because Cleopatra had judged it more prudent to send him against the king of Arabia, that the two kings might mutually weaken one another.

But with a daring amounting to genius, Herod rushed to the help of Didius, the governor of Syria, in his attack upon a band of Antony's gladiators; had the aged Hyrcanus II executed on an highly improbable charge of conspiracy; committed Mariamme to the care of one Sohemus, with the same command as that he had previously given Joseph; and went to meet the new master of the republic. When brought into the presence of Octavius, Herod laid aside nothing of royal state except his diadem, told of his services to Antony, boasted that he had not deserted him, and finally left it to Octavius to say whether or not he should be allowed to continue as a servant of Rome. Octavius saw the value of the man, reestablished him as king, and after the two had visited Egypt together, gave him back Jericho, and also added to his territories the cities of Gadara, Hippos, Samaria, Gaza, Anthedon, Joppa, and Strato's Tower.

But again Herod was to be tormented by quarrels among the women of his family. Salome and Cypros, stung by the contempt of Mariamme, waited only an opportunity to cause her downfall. The moment came when, after a year of stormy life, Herod was finally driven furious by his wife's contempt and reproaches. Then again did Salome accuse her of infidelity, and in a paroxysm of rage and jealousy Herod ordered (28 B.C.) Mariamme to execution. Alexandra, in an attempt to preserve herself, flooded her daughter with taunts and insults, but the proud and beautiful woman met her death without even a change of colour a worthy descendant of her house.

No sooner was his wife dead than Herod became insane with grief. He gave up the administration of the state, commanded his servants to act as if Mariamme were still alive, plunged into all sorts of excesses, and, if the rabbinical legend is to be believed, kept Mariamme's body by him, preserved in honey. So critical did his condition become that, in anticipation of his death, Alexandra undertook to seize the kingdom for herself and her grandsons; but her efforts were reported to Herod, and he promptly had her executed (28 B.C.). Thereupon he seems to have partially recovered; but throughout his life he was subject to attacks of melancholy during which he was blood-thirsty and tyrannical. Three years later, again at the instigation of Salome, who had married Costobar, he sought out and executed the sons of Babas, the last representatives of the Asmonean house, together with Costobar himself, who had offered them an asylum for twelve years. After this he was without rivals, except those of his own family.

The succeeding period of twenty years furnishes little to relate except a record of lavish building, the story of new domestic tragedies and growing Pharisaism. Its earlier and happier, portion was taken up with Herod's efforts to imitate Augustus as a builder. He had early rebuilt the citadel of the temple, renaming it, in honour of his friend Antony, Antonia, and later he added a theatre and an amphitheatre as well as impregnable towers at Jerusalem. He celebrated games every fourth year in honour of Augustus, and hung up various inscriptions and trophies in his honour. This Roman zeal of their king, together with his constant innovations, aroused the more fanatical Jews to desperation, and a conspiracy was formed to kill Herod. It was betrayed, and its members were executed. It showed Herod, however, the danger that lay in his position, and he immediately began to fortify and garrison various parts of the country in readiness for a revolt. Sebaste, Caesarea, Gaba in Galilee, and Heshbon in Perea were among the military posts he thus established, while he also built castles in other parts of the country, like Herodium southeast of Bethlehem, (Frank Mountain), and Herodium in Arabia, or rebuilt Asmonean strongholds that had been dismantled, like Alexandrium, Machaerus, Masada, and Hyrcania. In the case of Sebaste and Caesarea, he built really magnificent cities, the ruins of the former (Sebustieh) even to-day being considerable. Caesarea, in building which twelve years were spent, became the most important seaport south of Ptolemais, and boasted huge moles, quays, towers, sewers, temples, colonnades, palaces, as well as an amphitheatre, a theatre, and a hippodrome. Like Sebaste it was named in honour of Augustus, whose temple high above the city commanded the entire region. Nor did his passion for building stop with military necessities. In the Jordan valley he built the cities of Antipatris and Phasaelis, named in honour of his father and unfortunate brother, and a citadel at Jericho, which was named for his mother, Cypros. In the maritime plain he rebuilt Anthedon and named it Agrippaeum, in honour of his friend Agrippa, while he also erected temples, colonnades, or other public buildings in most cities he visited, but especially in Antioch, Rhodes, Nicopolis, Chios, Ascalon, Tyre, Sidon, Banias, Byblus, Berytus, Tripolis, Ptolemais, Damascus, Athens, and Sparta.

Herod's regard for heathen customs, displayed in much of this building, is also evidenced by the games he established at Caesarea and Jerusalem, by his gifts toward maintaining the Olympic games, and by his choice of Greeks to administer his affairs and to act as tutors for his sons. He is even said to have studied Greek philosophy under Nicholas of Damascus, his litterateur and orator. At the same time he followed the customs of Rome by building himself a strongly fortified palace in the Upper City at Jerusalem, in laying out parks, and breeding pigeons.

At the same time that he was thus winning popularity in the Greek world, Herod did not cease to be a king of the Jews. His internal improvements were worthy of the man he copied. The water supply of Jerusalem was improved, the robber bands of Trachonitis were controlled by three thousand Idumean colonists, the miseries of famine were alleviated by public works employing fifty thousand men, and aid was given to other sufferers until even the royal plate was sold. Twice did he reduce the taxes, once in 20 B.C. by a third, and once in 14 B.C. by a fourth. In addition, the country was kept in peace, robbers were everywhere attacked, the frontier was rigorously guarded. So successful was he in his administration that Augustus gave him successively Trachonitis, Auranitis, Batanea, and the tetrarchy of Zenodorus, which included Banias, while his brother Pheroras was appointed tetrarch of Perea, and the procurator of Syria was ordered to consult with the king in all important matters.

Such good administration won him also the favour of the people. If they murmured somewhat at his lavish devotion to heathen life, they appreciated the regard for their prejudices concerning graven images shown in his coins and buildings, as well as the political necessity under which he was placed. Even more did they appreciate the substantial aid that such friendship enabled Herod to gain for the Jews, not only in Judea but in the Dispersion. The Pharisees themselves might praise a ruler who respected their opinions, paused to prove the absence of impiety in trophies, demanded circumcision of a suitor for his sister's hand, scrupulously observed the sanctity of the temple and its courts, and whose accusers before Agrippa and Augustus were the Arabians and the heathen citizens of Gadara. Even his enemies could plead little against him beyond severity in the interests of order, and the most fanatical must have honoured a ruler who excused many of their scribes from taking an oath of allegiance, and who especially honoured the Essenes. It is true, on the other hand, that he had greatly weakened the Sanhedrin by the massacre of its Sadducean members with which he began his reign, but there is no good reason for doubting that it continued both as a sort of Pharisaic academy whose decisions were final in matters of religion, and as a court before whom Herod himself could cite the unfortunate Hyrcanus II. Even if he removed and appointed the high priests arbitrarily, his action was offset by the magnificent temple which in 20 B.C. he began to erect in place of the one ascribed to Zerubbabel, as well as by the regard for the priests as a class he exhibited during the eighteen months of its building, and his own observance of the building's sanctity.

But whatever popularity such facts as these imply, was lost during the last years of Herod's life. Again family troubles aroused the worst side of his nature, and his family and the Pharisees alike suffered. As he grew older, he grew less tolerant of his people's prejudices. Understand them he most certainly did; but either confidence in his own power, or some insanity resulting from his domestic tragedy, led him repeatedly to irritate and enrage them in a way altogether impossible for him during his better years. It is in these later years that one must seek the obscure beginnings of that Zealot party which was later to prove so terrible an agent of revolt. Unlike the Essenes, the Zealots seem to have sprung directly from the Pharisees, from whom they came to differ largely in this one respect: despairing of any Messiah, and impatient for the coming of the kingdom of God, they tired of faith and patience and looked to revolution. Patriotism with them was synonymous with action. They would "see the judgments and all the curses of their enemies." It is their spirit that appeared in the group of three thousand Pharisees who refused to take the oath of allegiance to Herod and the emperor, and it is easy to see members of the party also in the mob of fanatics under the two rabbis, Judas and Mattathias, who tore down the eagle Herod had carved over the entrance to the temple.

But apart from his growing severity toward his people, Herod's last years were full of misery. The absence of any clear law governing succession to the throne, and the consequent opportunity for plots and counter-plots in favour of some one of the king's numerous sons, doubtless explain much of the tragedy that marked these years, but along with them must be placed the character of Herod himself. The mad determination not to surrender his throne before his death; the fierce suspicion that, first aroused by treachery among them he loved best, embraced an ever-increasing number of those nearest him; the tyrannical control of his people; all sprang from a character as unrestrained in its passions as in its energies.

His difficulties with his family were of long standing, but became acute when in order to curb the arrogance of Alexander and Aristobulus, his sons by Mariamme, he caused his eldest son Antipater to be brought from Galilee, where he had been living in semi-banishment. The two young men, proud of their Asmonean descent, bore their disgrace ill, and soon became indiscreet, even if not disloyal in speech. The situation was complicated by the enmities and jealousies of the various women in the royal household — Salome, the king's sister, Glaphyra, the wife of Alexander, Bernice, the daughter of Salome, the wife of Aristobulus, and the various wives of Herod himself, while through it all ran the poisonous influence of Antipater, set upon the death of the sons of Mariamme.

The storm broke first in B.C. 12, and Herod then took Aristobulus and Alexander to Rome, to accuse them before the emperor, but Augustus had brought about a reconciliation. Two years later, certain eunuchs, under torture, confessed that Alexander had made contemptuous remarks about Herod, and even was plotting with his brother Aristobulus against him. Herod at once arrested Alexander, tortured and killed his friends, and, as Alexander, doubtless in hopes of Roman interference, endeavoured to incite him to greater madness, became almost insane with fear and suspicion. Yet just when affairs were most desperate, the father-in-law of Alexander, Archelaus of Cappadocia, could bring about a reconciliation between the father and son by feigning to malign Alexander. Herod's fatherly instincts were yet too strong to endure such an attack upon the child of Mariamme, and he restored Alexander to favour, showering Archelaus with all sorts of presents! For a few months the family lived in peace. Herod was engaged in punishing a wily Arab who had defaulted payment on some bond, and, thanks to this rascal's monetary influence at the imperial court, found himself in disfavour with Augustus. So far did the misunderstanding go that the emperor wrote Herod that "whereas of old he had treated Herod as his friend, he should now treat him as his subject." But even while affairs were in this condition the brothers were again accused of treason, and when, through the efforts of Nicholas of Damascus, Herod was restored to favour, Augustus gave him full power to deal with his sons as he saw fit. A few weeks later they were tried and condemned before a court at Berytus (Beirut) and (B.C. 7) strangled at Sebaste. Thereupon Antipater, in complete control of his father, went to Rome to await the old king's death.

But the fearful drama was not yet complete. Herod turned fiercely upon the Pharisees, and was engaging in something like persecution, when, thanks to the revelations of Salome, he suddenly discovered the true character of Antipater. He ordered him back to Judea, had him tried, condemned, and imprisoned. Later, again with the consent of Augustus, he had the wretch executed. Ten days later he himself died, dividing his kingdom among three of his sons: Archelaus, to whom he gave Judea, with the title of king; Herod Antipas, to whom he gave Galilee and Perea, with the title of tetrarch; and Philip, to whom he gave the northeastern districts, also with the title of tetrarch.

He had reigned thirty-seven years.

CHAPTER XI: ARCHELAUS (4 B.C.-6 A.D.)

BEFORE Herod's will could serve as a basis for the new administrations of his sons it had to be reviewed and confirmed by Augustus. As a result, Judea was left for months without any settled government, exposed to every form of disorder. At once there appeared the Pharisees' hatred of a royal house, and their determination to reestablish their doctrinaire Utopia of a theocracy of scribes. Disturbances broke out almost immediately after the gorgeous funeral Archelaus gave his father at Herodium. Archelaus had been saluted as king; but although he had taken his seat upon a golden throne, he had been careful not to accept the title. None the less, the bodies of the people came to him demanding reforms in taxation, the release of those imprisoned by Herod, and the abolition of taxes on sales. Archelaus agreed to these demands, but the more extreme members of the Pharisees were unwilling to let the opportunity pass without obtaining revenge. Shortly before the death of Herod, two prominent rabbis, Judas and Mattathias, had incited their students to tear down the golden eagle over the great gate of the temple. Herod had thereupon caused the ringleaders to be burnt. The Pharisees now demanded the punishment of those persons who had been instrumental in the executions. Lacking any authority for reversing the action of his father, Archelaus very properly endeavoured to delay action until after his position had been made certain by Caesar. But all his efforts proved unavailing. The popular leaders continued to excite the people, and at the Passover following the death of Herod the Jews assembled in crowds at the temple, threatening revolution. Archelaus, fearing that they might do some irreparable damage to the state, had his troops attack them, and when the crowds dispersed to their homes they had lost three thousand of their number.

Thinking that order had been restored, Archelaus, accompanied by his friends, his aunt Salome, and many of his other relatives, went off to Rome, leaving his brother Philip as his representative in Judea. Shortly afterward Antipas also went up to Rome, with the purpose of persuading Augustus to ratify that will of Herod by which he had been made king. During the absence of Archelaus the country was cursed with a succession of Jewish fanatics, Galilean robbers, who declared themselves kings, and

Roman peculators. Judea became full of anarchy. The propraetor of Syria, Varus, after having subdued one uprising at Jerusalem, returned to Antioch, leaving one legion under Sabinus, his procurator, to maintain order. But Sabinus not only had little but police powers, but far worse, soon proved to be more eager to get posses-sion of the treasures left by Herod than to check the rapidly increasing revolt. At the feast of Pentecost the Jews renewed hostilities and seized the temple area. There from the roofs of the cloisters they maintained a desperate and successful fight against the Romans; until the latter set the cloisters on fire. All of the Jews then perished, and the Romans got possession of most of the treasures of the temple, Sabinus openly taking four hundred talents. The revolt was finally put down by Varus with great slaughter, two thousand Jews being crucified.

While thus Judea was in the greatest disorder, a most extraordinary gathering of Jews and their rulers was being held in Rome. The Pharisees now attempted lawfully what their lunatic followers had sought by rebellion. With the permission of Varus an embassy of fifty prominent Jews proceeded to Rome to endeavour to prevent the appointment of Archelaus as king. There they were joined by eight thousand members of the Jewish colony in Rome, and sought to get Judea incorporated in the province of Syria in hopes that they might have more liberty to live by their own laws.

At the suggestion of Varus, Philip also went to Rome to aid Archelaus, or to have some share in the distribution of Herod's estate.

Augustus gave the petitioners several audiences, and at last practically confirmed the last will of Herod. Archelaus was to have Judea, Samaria, and Idumea, with a tribute of six hundred talents. He was to have at first the title of ethnarch, and later, in case he governed well, the title of king. Herod Antipas was given Galilee and Perea, with the annual tribute of two hundred talents and the title of tetrarch. Philip was given the same title, the regions of Gaulanitis, Auranitis, Trachonitis, Batanea, Banias, and Iturea, with an income of one hundred talents. The cities of Gaza, Gadara, and Hippos were, however, excluded from this division and made subject directly to Syria. Herod's provisions for Salome were confirmed, and in addition she was given a palace at Ascalon. The other relatives of Herod received the bequests contained in his will. Augustus further made handsome presents of money to Herod's two daughters, and divided the sum left himself among the dead king's sons.

The character of the ethnarch, Archelaus, was, in most respects, like that of Herod, without its better qualities. Like his father, he was a builder. He restored the royal palace at Jericho, which had been burned during the disturbances that had occurred while he had been in Rome, and planted and irrigated new palm groves in its vicinity. He also built a town in the Jordan valley, near Phasaelis, which he called after himself, Archelais. Like his father also, he dealt wantonly with the high priests, removing one and appointing another, twice during his reign of ten years. He still further shocked the sensibilities of the people by marrying the widow of his half-brother, Alexander, by whom she had had children. Glaphyra, however, died soon after her marriage, after having had a dream sufficiently striking to be recorded by Josephus.

The reign of Archelaus is described by Josephus, briefly, as being barbarous and tyrannical, although he gives us no basis for the characterization except the facts just stated. But that he is correct seems clear, from the fact that in A.D. 6 the principal men of Judea and Samaria, together with the sons of Herod, accused him, before Augustus, of mismanaging his territory. Augustus was very angry, and immediately despatched the representative of Archelaus in Rome to summon him to trial. The messenger hurried Archelaus from a banquet to the imperial court, where he was condemned, A.D. 6, and sentenced to the confiscation of his property, and to banishment at Vienne, in Gaul, where he probably died. Quirinius was sent to make a census of the taxable property of Judea, as a first step in its organization as a province. Such organization was completed when Idumea, Samaria, and Judea were put under Coponius as procurator.

But this reorganization was not accomplished without bloodshed. The census, hateful alike on religious and political grounds, met with fanatical opposition. It is true that the Jews, as a whole, did not revolt, and singularly enough the disturbance broke out in Galilee, which was not subject to the census. But the Zealots — whom now for the first time Josephus describes — were not over-sensitive to consistency, and under one Judas a Galilean and one Sadduc a Pharisee rose against their new masters in full belief that God would aid them in achieving liberty. Josephus himself sees in them the originators of the war of 66-70. Be that as it may, this religious and political outbreak was the expression of the new party spirit among the Jews. The Zealots, like the Pharisees, awaited a kingdom of God, a Messiah, and a new Israel, but their kingdom was to be won by the sword — not, it should be noticed, however, from persecutors like Antiochus Epiphanes, but from purely political masters who allowed the Jews every conceivable religious liberty.

CHAPTER XII: PALESTINE UNDER THE ROMANS AND THE TETRARCHS

EXCLUSIVE of the Greek cities, Palestine was broken into three separate administrative districts, the province of Judea and the tetrarchies of Herod Antipas and Philip — a division that seems to have outlasted the Jewish nation itself.

1. Of these three districts, the most important in all respects was the province of Judea, over which were the procurators. It was composed of three parts, each historically distinct from each other. Samaria lay between Judea and Galilee, corresponding roughly to the ancient Northern Kingdom of Israel, except that it no longer included the plain of Esdraelon, Jenin being its northern border. It apparently extended from the Jordan to the maritime plain, but its northern boundary was never long fixed. Josephus gives the Acrabattene toparchy, the village Annath or Borceas, and Korea, as on the border. It was and is a fertile region, and although small, its area being even less than that of Galilee, like Judea, it was "full of people" whose history has already been seen to have been closely interwoven with that of the Jews proper.

Judea, the most important division of the country, and that which gave its name to the province, extended from Samaria to the desert, and from the Jordan to the maritime plain, the cities of which, even Joppa and Jamnia, thoroughly Jewish though they were, not being counted as a part of it. Its area was approximately two thousand square miles. It was divided into eleven toparchies, at the head of which was Jerusalem, although the official residence of the procurator was Caesarea. Jerusalem, alone of all the towns of Judea, was a city in anything like the Graeco-Roman sense. The nature of these toparchies is not altogether clear, but probably they consisted of a town and its surrounding country. The smaller towns of Judea do not seem to have been very much organised, and were probably dependent upon some larger city or metropolis. If this conjecture be correct, we have another parallel between the Graeco-Egyptian and the Graeco-Jewish administration. These villages had their own councils or sanhedrins which tried civil and less important criminal cases, and were probably administered by "village-clerks" precisely as in Egypt. The relation of

Jerusalem to these toparchies was something more than that of a merely nominal head. Itself the one great city out of the twenty-nine which Judea boasted, its Council, or Sanhedrin, not only was the court of appeal, but its officials collected the tribute paid to the Romans. Its position is to be seen also in the fact that in the great rebellion it organised all Judea and, at least imperfectly, Galilee against their enemy. This superiority, however, did not extend over the Greek cities of Judea, which were either like Caesarea directly attached to the province of Syria, or held as the private property of some favoured person.

Idumea was the district lying to the south of Judea proper, including the Negeb and the southern Shephelah. John Hyrcanus conquered it, and compelled its inhabitants to receive the law of Moses and circumcision. Notwithstanding the fact that its inhabitants were regarded as the descendants of Isaac only through Esau and that the Herodian family originated within it, Idumea was treated as Jewish, since descendants of three generations were regarded as real Jews. In the time of Christ this was increasingly true, and during the War, the Idumeans were among the most fanatical of all the revolutionists. It is not possible to discover the exact political relations of Idumea to the province, but it would seem to have been treated as a toparchy.

These three little districts were joined into Judea, an imperial province of the second rank, governed by a procurator who was of the equestrian rank, Strictly speaking, Judea was not a part of Syria, although in one or two exceptional cases the legate of that province seems to have possessed some power over the procurators. But apart from these exceptional cases the procurator was vested with full powers. Primarily a fiscal agent, his office naturally kept him at the head of the administration of the taxes and the customs. Of the two, the taxes were more directly under his control, although under the empire the Roman governors were no longer able to abuse the provincials as under the republic. In fact, they had become salaried officials, and whatever taxes were collected — in the case of Judea, probably six hundred talents — were expended as far as necessary upon the province itself for public improvements like roads, harbours, public buildings, and the remainder was sent to the imperial treasury (fiscus). It was probably for this collection of taxes that Judea had been divided into toparchies, and to the sanhedrin of each was probably assigned the duty of collecting the tax levied upon it. These taxes, however, were no longer farmed, but collected by imperial officials. Naturally the procurator of Judea could levy no taxes upon the tetrarchies of Antipas and Philip,

But if the taxes were officially collected, the customs were farmed. They were of almost every conceivable sort, export duties, import duties, octroi, bridge and harbour duties, market taxes, tax on salt, and were sold out to speculators, who in turn sold their rights to various collectors. The men who actually did the collecting the publicans (mokhes) of the New Testament were thus exposed to the strongest temptation to misuse their position, and no class of men was ever more cordially hated. However much the local authorities might attempt to regulate the import, the despised collectors were always able to levy blackmail and practise extortion.

In addition to his fiscal duties the procurator had military and judicial powers that easily made him master of Judea. Except at feasts, only a single cohort was stationed at Jerusalem. His troops consisted almost exclusively of mercenaries, chiefly Samaritans, a fact that did not make toward good feeling. As a judge he had the power of life and death, appeal to the emperor being granted only in case of Roman citizens, and then only after formal protest had been made. Yet the number of cases actually brought before the procurator was probably small, for most would doubtless be settled in one of the toparchical sanhedrins, or in the great Sanhedrin of Jerusalem, where the Jewish law would be understood. Crimes involving capital punishment were, however, in his hands, although it is not quite certain at what date the right was thus restricted.

In general the establishment of the Roman administration probably affected Jewish society but little. It may even have been acceptable to the Pharisees, if, as Josephus says, the government fell really into the hands of native aristocracy with the high priest at its head. The Jews were indeed required to take the oath of allegiance to each new emperor, and the procurator, except at feasts, kept the robe of the high priest locked up in the castle of Antonia, but such requirements were more than offset by the religious liberty given the Jews, the guaranteed sanctity of the temple, and the general leniency shown their intense religious feeling. Apart from the Zealots it is probable that there was but a minority of the inhabitants of Judea that did not assent heartily to the daily sacrifices of two lambs and an ox for the welfare of the emperor. Such examples of tolerance as the recognition of the Sabbath, the omission of the emperor's head on the copper coinage of the country, the leaving of military standards outside

Jerusalem, the recognition of the Jews' right to kill even a Roman citizen who went beyond the court of the Gentiles in the temple, are as creditable to the Romans as indicative of the extraordinary religious fervour of the Jews themselves. Indeed, from the days of Julius Caesar the Jews had enjoyed special favours from the Romans, who, it will be remembered, seldom interfered with a conquered people's customs and institutions further than was absolutely necessary in the interest of good administration.

In the case of Judea the native courts or sanhedrins were also left in possession of considerable powers of local jurisdiction and administration, and the people were thus allowed large opportunity for pursuing the practice as well as the study of the Law.

It is here that one meets the culminating institution of legalistic Judaism — the Sanhedrin of Jerusalem. If the various rabbinical traditions concerning its origin be disregarded, the Sanhedrin of Jerusalem may be said to have been essentially the Gerousia of that city with changed powers and character. As merely a town-council its powers had sensibly diminished from the death of Simon, and it had become increasingly judicial and academic in character. At the same time it had doubtless grown in the estimation of the people at large, and, as it grew predominantly Pharisaic, its prestige and influence still more increased. Under Aristobulus II and Antigonus it is true its membership was largely from the Sadducees, but the massacre of forty-five of its members by Herod immediately after his victory over Antigonus again opened the way for Pharisaic predominance. Thus under Herod the Sanhedrin first became the creature of the king, ready even to condemn the unfortunate Hyrcanus, but lost practically all of such administrative powers as it still retained. With the establishment of the provincial government, it regained many of such powers, and, in addition, became the supreme court for all cases of importance civil, criminal, and religious under the Mosaic law. That it had any jurisdiction in Galilee during the reign of Herod Antipas seems unlikely, although its decisions on legal points, especially concerning marriage, divorce, genealogies, heresies, and the calendar, would undoubtedly be received as final by all Jews. In Judea proper it could make arrests, try and condemn criminals to any punishment except death, without any ratification on the part of the procurator. In all capital cases condemnation could not be pronounced until after a night had passed, but no such restriction applied to acquittal. All decisions were apparently made by a majority, but in convictions this must not be less than two.

The Sanhedrin met on Mondays and Thursdays in its own building, which probably stood on the west side of the temple mount. It was composed of seventy-two members of pure Hebrew descent; twenty-three constituting a quorum. How the members were appointed is uncertain, but they were inducted into the body by the laying on of hands. They were not all of equal rank; the members of the high priestly families being naturally the more important. The other members of the body were called scribes, or simply elders. The latter two classes were doubtless Pharisees. The Sanhedrin seems to have been organised with the high priest as president, and with the Committee of Ten, so common in Graeco-Roman towns.

Of the early procurators there is very little known. They had the power of removing and appointing high, priests, but judged Jews according to Jewish law. Their office was not an easy one, and the fanatical hatred of the Jews and Samaritans was constantly leading to outbreaks requiring severe punishment. Of them all, Pontius Pilate is best known, not merely from the gospels, but from Philo and Josephus. The former describes him as of an "unbending and recklessly hard character," while the latter gives various incidents of his alleged oppression. At this distance, however, one of these acts seems to have been due to inexperience; and the others the use of temple treasures to build an aqueduct, and the punishment of the Samaritans for what certainly looks like an incipient revolution seem those of a man very much in earnest to maintain order and give a good administration. The fact that Tiberius, who was especially attentive to the provinces, left him in office for ten years, is distinctly in his favour a fact that his condemnation under Caligula does not seriously affect.

2. Altogether independent of the procurators were the tetrarchies given the two sons of Herod. Of these two, that of Philip embraced the territory lying between the Yarmuk, the Jordan, Mount Hermon, and Damascus and the desert, but its boundaries are very difficult to locate exactly. It was composed of a number of small districts (Batanea, Trachonitis, Gaulanitis, Iturea, Auranitis), which had been conquered by Jewish rulers, especially Herod I, or which had been given Herod I by Rome. This heterogeneous tetrarchy, after having been raised to a kingdom by Caligula, continued its political life after the destruction of Jerusalem.

The tetrarch Philip (4 B.C.-34 A.D.) was the most respectable of the three brothers who succeeded Herod. His territory was not Jewish, and was far less productive than that of either Archelaus or Antipas, yet he seems to have been content to live within it, especially seeking to administer justice. One of the most peaceful pictures of these years is that of Philip travelling through his rough dominions attended by a few chosen friends, and sitting as judge in the market-places of the cities and towns, or wherever a case had to be tried. Like his father, he was fond of building. Banias was made into a noble city, with rights of asylum, which he named Caesarea (Philippi), and on the east bank of the Jordan, just above its entrance into the Lake of Galilee, he made the village of Bethsaida into a city, which, in honour of the daughter of Augustus, he called Julias. Removed from the influences of the Jewish life, he grew increasingly Hellenistic, and again like his father, built many temples to the heathen gods. He seems to have had some interest in scientific matters, for it is related of him that he proved (at least to the satisfaction of his own time) that the springs at Banias mark the emergence of an underground river, by throwing chaff into the pool of Phiala. Further than this, little is known of his reign, except that he stamped his image on his coins, which, although not unprecedented in the history of the Jews, is sufficient to show his Hellenistic sympathies. At his death, his territory, though, still controlling its revenues, was added to Syria, but later was given by Caligula to Herod Agrippa I (37 A.D.), with the title of king.

3. Much more important was the tetrarchy of Herod Antipas, consisting of Galilee and Perea.

In popular speech, Galilee was divided into two parts — Upper and Lower. Upper Galilee is much higher and more mountainous, some of its peaks reaching nearly four thousand feet; while Lower Galilee has rolling hills and fine valleys in which sycamores grow — a prime distinction in the Talmud. As, however, the two were politically a unit, it is hardly necessary to retain the division.

On the north Galilee was bounded by Tyre, the line running approximately through Tell-el-kadi to the Litani; on the east by the Jordan and the Sea of Galilee and again the Jordan; on the south by the region of Scythopolis and Samaria, the line running along the southern edge of Esdraelon; and on the west by the regions of Tyre, which included Carmel and Ptolemais. Altogether it measured fifty or sixty miles north and south, and from twenty-five to thirty-five east and west, its area being about sixteen hundred square miles. It was an exceedingly prosperous region, full of vineyards and gardens, villages and cities, while its beautiful lake — the

Sea of Galilee — had upon its northwestern side the plain of Gennesaret, regarded by Josephus as "an ambitions effort of nature doing violence to herself in bringing together plants of discordant habits, with an admirable rivalry of the seasons, each as it were, asserting her rights to the soil; a spot where grapes and figs grew during ten months without intermission, while the other varieties of fruit ripened the year round." Its capital was Sepphoris, until Herod Antipas transferred that honour to his new city of Tiberias. Under the later Maccabees and Herod I, Galilee had been a part of the kingdom of the Jews, but after the death of Herod I it was separated from the rest of Palestine and given as a tetrarchy to Herod Antipas. Thereafter it retained to some degree its identity, being treated probably as an administrative unit; for we find it added entire to the kingdom of Herod Agrippa I, and at the time of the Jewish war assigned to Josephus for organisation. There is, however, no certain evidence that it was ever treated as a separate procuratorial district.

Galilee was inhabited by Gentiles and Jews, although the latter undoubtedly predominated. They are called Galileans, but whenever contrasted with other peoples, like the Romans, they are called Jews, as, indeed, are also the Samaritans and Pereans. But it should be remembered that in the time of Jesus this Jewish element had not been long resident in Galilee. Whatever colonists had settled there prior to the Maccabean revolt had been removed by Simon. It was probably not until after Aristobulus conquered and circumcised the Itureans, or North Galileans, that the tide of Jewish colonisation really set in again. In the days of Josephus the region was densely populated, and judging from the ruins surrounding the Sea of Galilee it is difficult to believe that he is exaggerating seriously when he declares that it possessed three walled cities and two hundred and four villages. The Galileans were a sturdy, impulsive people, with the virtues of all colonists, inured to war, ready for resistance to oppression, and although thorough Jews in their devotion to the Law and the temple, without the arid fanaticism of the Judeans. In many particulars their moral life was more healthy than that of the inhabitants of other portions of Palestine, and as regards marriage public sentiment was much purer. Farmers and fishermen, they were marked by considerable idealism, for it is worth noticing that Galileans were always ready to accept Messianic claims. No region was more punctual in the observance of the Sabbath and the feasts. At the same time they were much more than the Judeans in constant relations with Graeco-Roman civilisation, and this perhaps gave them a freer and broader life than that of their southern brethren.

Grouped with Galilee was the somewhat larger region of Perea. It lay on the east of Jordan and extended from the Yarmuk to the Arnon, and from the regions of Gerasa, Philadelphia, and the desert to the Jordan. Within it, though politically independent, were many of the cities of the Decapolis, but this fact did not prevent its being considered as second to Judea alone in the purity of its Judaism. Politically it was of but little importance.

Herod Antipas, to whom these prosperous regions were entrusted, although far from being Herod's equal, had more of his father's abilities than either of his two brothers. He is called a king in the gospels; and, although the title is not strictly correct, it probably represents popular terminology. As in the case of his brother, Philip, we are left in doubt as to the course of his long reign (4 B.C.-39 A.D.), Josephus telling us but little except certain gossipy details. Like his father, he was a great builder. Sepphoris, the most important city of Galilee, which had suffered at the hands of the robber chief, Judas, he once more surrounded with a wall and made again the metropolis. He also walled the city of Betharamptha, in which the palace of Herod had been destroyed during the anarchy following his death, renaming it Livias, or Julias, in honour of the emperor's wife. He seems also to have done some similar service to Cos and Delos, as tablets in his honour have been found in those islands. But the most important of such undertakings was his building of the new city of Tiberias, on the western bank of the Sea of Galilee, not far from the celebrated hot springs. The ruins of this city, which yet remain stretched along the lake and the highlands above it, show but imperfectly its original importance. To judge from the order of events as recorded by Josephus, Herod built it after the coming of Pilate, as procurator of Judea (26 A.D.), naming it in honour of the Emperor Tiberius. It had a number of large buildings, including a stadium; a royal palace, ornamented with the golden tile and figures of animals; and a great proseuche, or prayer house, of the Jews. As appears from its ruins, it was surrounded by walls, with bastions extending into the lake, and had colonnaded streets. In organisation it was thoroughly Greek, having a council of six hundred members, with an archon at its head, and a Committee of Ten, together with other officials. Its population was mixed. As it was partly built over sepulchres, it was at first shunned by the stricter Jews; but many were compelled to settle in it by Herod Antipas, and others were attracted by gifts of homes and lands, and by the time of the great war it was evidently filled with fanatical Jews. So rapidly did it grow, and so much was it in favour with Antipas, that he made it his capital, superior even to Sepphoris, though it was not as large.

The character of Herod Antipas is summed up by the word of Jesus, — "fox." Singularly enough, we have an illustration of his cunning. At one time he accompanied Vitellius on an embassy to Artabanus, king of Parthia. The meeting was held in a rich tent, pitched by Herod on a bridge over the Euphrates. As soon as the desired treaty was concluded, in order to forestall Vitellius and be the first to report the good news to Tiberius, Herod hurried off a full report to the emperor. That of Vitellius was therefore unnecessary, and Herod may be supposed to have gained in the estimation of Tiberius. But he made Vitellius his enemy, as he was to discover later to his cost. The same trait of character appears in his attitude toward the Jews, to whom, much more than in the case of Philip, it was necessary to be gracious. Here he followed closely in the footsteps of his father, balancing his friendship for Rome and heathen customs by his attendance upon the feasts at Jerusalem. He put no image on his coins, and joined in a protest against Pilate for having set up a votive shield in the temple. As far as we can judge from the material at our disposal, the Pharisees never regarded him with the same suspicion and hatred they had shown his father during his later years.

It was characteristic of his house that misfortune should reach him through his domestic relations. Antipas had been married to the daughter of the king of Arabia, but on one occasion, when in Rome, he had fallen in love with Herodias, the wife of the Herod who lived as a private citizen at the capital. The fact that she was his own niece caused no hesitation, and they had arranged to be married as soon as Antipas could rid himself of his legal wife. In some way, however, this wife learned of his plans and fled to her father, who thereupon made war upon his faithless son-in-law. Aiitipas was defeated through treachery, and complained to Tiberius, who ordered Vitellius to assist him. Tiberius died, however, before Vitellius had fairly begun the campaign, and the expedition was given up. Herodias had, in the meantime, divorced her husband and married Antipas. Later she had seen her brother, Agrippa I, made king over the former tetrarchy of Philip (37 A.D.), and had grown ambitious for her new husband to be made king also. With considerable difficulty she persuaded Antipas to ask the emperor Caligula for the title, but he met with an unexpected reply. The preparations made for carrying on his war with Arabia gave Agrippa I an opportunity to get revenge for certain quarrels, and he wrote the emperor that Antipas was preparing to revolt. As the unhappy tetrarch was unable to deny that his arsenals were full of weapons, Caligula refused to listen to explanations, and forthwith banished him to Lyons, whither Herodias accompanied him.

4. Interspersed within the regions of Galilee, Perea, and the tetrarchy of Philip, was the Decapolis. It would be incorrect to speak of it as a region or district, for it was nothing more politically than a confederation of great Graeco-Roman cities. Scythopolis, its capital, was on the west of Jordan, and on the various roads that spread out like the sticks of a fan from the fords and bridge it controlled, were Pella, Gadara, Hippos, Dium, Gerasa, Philadelphia, Raphana, Kanatha, and at one time Damascus. The union of these ten cities, for military and commercial purposes, was probably brought about during the time of Pompey, and although the Romans gave Hippos and Gadara to Herod, and the latter city seems to have joined in the great revolt against Rome, the league maintained itself for centuries, and at the time of Ptolemy embraced eighteen towns, most of them lying in the region between Damascus and the Yarmuk. Each of these cities had a considerable territory attached to it, and was thus an example of the city-state; and although several of them were in the midst of some of the main political divisions already described, they were not subject to either procurator or tetrarch. For this reason their territories were not continuous, and it is impossible to speak of a "region of the Decapolis" in anything more than a popular sense. But it should be further noted that not merely in the Decapolis were there cities clearly differing from Jewish towns and called distinctly Hellenistic by Josephus. All over the region west of the Jordan were such, cities to be found. Ptolemais, Dora, Caesarea, Apollonia, Jamnia, Azotus, Ascalon, Gaza, Anthedon, Phasaelis, and others crowded along the coast; Antipatris and Sebaste lay further inland, and Archelais, in the Jordan valley. Each city had some dependent region, and in all of them it is probable were Jewish quarters, as in Alexandria. Several like Caesarea, Sebaste, Tiberias, and Gaba, had been built by Jewish rulers, but they were organised after Greek rather than Jewish models, and were filled with a vigorous anti-Semitism that needed only incipient anarchy to break out in massacres, or even, as in the case of Caesarea, to occasion revolution.

The presence of this energetic heathenism in politics and social life produced no small effect upon Jewish life and thought. It is perhaps true, although outside the Sadducees and such men as Josephus evidence is not abundant, that the new Hellenism exercised something of a liberalising influence. Certainly the great mass of the Palestinian Jews spoke if they did not read Greek, and Hellenism made itself felt in other directions, notably in architecture, music, commerce, and money. Possibly, even in literature the same was true of Palestine as of the Dispersion, where we find a considerable number of Jewish authors, chiefly historians and poets.

But it was among those Jews who lived outside of Palestine that the positive influences of Graeco-Roman civilisation are mostly seen. From the time of Antiochus III, indeed from that of Alexander the Great, the Jews had been regarded as especially good colonists, and by the time of Augustus there was no city of any importance in the empire that did not possess its Jewish quarter. Sometimes, as at Alexandria, such colonies were very large; in other cities they could not even boast a place of prayer. Often, even if not generally, these "Grecians" as they were called, had some sort of political recognition, being organised into wards with ethnarchs of their own. They had their synagogues, their rabbis, their Law, and in Alexandria, it will be recalled, their temple. They were as devoted to Judaism as their brethren of Palestine, the "Hebrews," and their annual contributions to the maintenance of the temple at Jerusalem were enormous. Once, during his lifetime, every Jew hoped to attend the Passover at Jerusalem, and wherever he might live, whenever he prayed he turned his face toward the Holy City. Yet, despite this truly Jewish spirit, the members of the Dispersion were less narrow than the Palestinian Jews, and at times appear anti-Pharisaical. So far from wishing to set limits to Judaism, by proselyting, by interpreting their sacred books according to the spirit of various Greek philosophies, they endeavoured to bring about a universal Mosaism. In this they were by no means unsuccessful; but in the effort their own point of view was changed, and without any weakening of their national character there grew up among the Dispersion a new style of thinking and literature, in which Jewish and Greek elements are strangely mixed.

To some extent these influences affecting the Dispersion were transmitted by its members to the Jews in Palestine, but the influence exerted by the Greek population of the land itself was undoubtedly reactionary. However much the Palestinian Jew might feel the influence of Alexandria, the sight of so many thousand men and women indifferent to Jehovah and the Law; of idolatry with all its attendant customs; of contempt for the Sabbath and Jewish rites; even the occasional submission of individuals to circumcision or some less pronounced confession of proselytism; conspired to make the Pharisee and his devoted disciples the more zealous for their faith. Danger of a new period of degeneration, like that under Menelaus and Jason, there was none. Judaism grew sterner and the more exclusive under the pressure of Graeco-Roman life, and the scribes increased the number of cases in which any intercourse with a Gentile would defile a Jew. If politically the heathen possessed the land, religiously, Judaism under the inspiration of the Pharisees and Zealots was subject to no master except its God, and awaited in faith the establishment of His kingdom in the Holy Land. Jewish history was culminating in the Messianic hope.

CHAPTER XIII: THE MESSIANIC HOPE AND JESUS THE MESSIAH

IT is thus not difficult to picture the outer aspects of Jewish life in Palestine during the first half century of our era. Even if we disregard the cosmopolitan elements suggested by the Dispersion, it was no primitive society that filled Judea and the two tetrarchies. Cities crowded upon cities, bringing Jew and Greek together. Every nook and cranny of tillable ground bore its crop. The hills, whose thin soil made agriculture impossible, were covered with flocks; the Sea of Galilee was alive with fishing boats. Political agitation had been limited to "robbers" and the incipient party of the Zealots; while the tribes on the border, though occasionally defeating some native prince, did not venture seriously to disturb the Roman peace.

But the inner life of the people is not so easily grasped, for in most particulars it is as foreign to a Christian civilisation as to the men of Rome. Two contradictory dangers especially confront the student — that of overestimating and that of underestimating the religious element in Jewish life.

On the one hand, it is perfectly clear that the people at large did not share in the punctilious religious life of the Pharisees, however much they might admire it. In Palestine, as in modern lands, the proportion of those actively engaged in religious service was undoubtedly small. The fact that a village came a town when once it possessed ten men who agreed to be regular attendants upon the synagogue service, and the additional fact that later it became customary to pay these men for attending service, certainly do not heighten one's confidence in popular piety. It would seem, further, as if one synagogue sufficed for a town of considerable size. The am har-arets (people of the land) — the uneducated masses — were despised by the Pharisee, no't so much because of their poverty as because of their indifference to the Law and its discipline. They were sinners, whose presence defiled the person and the house of the Pharisee.

Nor is it improbable, though hardly to be proved, that there were those Jews who were filled more with the quiet spirit of the Second Isaiah rather than with the obtrusive piety of Pharisaism, — persons like the aged

Simeon and Anna, who waited for the consolation of Israel, untroubled by and perhaps indifferent to the mass of rabbinical laws.

Yet on the other hand, while ultra Judaism can be given too great an extent, its intensity can hardly be exaggerated. Legally centred about the temple and the high priest, its real soul was in scribism. Feasts, ritual, sacrifices, pilgrimages, tithes, Sabbaths, and fasts, these were all alike but expressions of the profound determination to keep God's law as expounded in the synagogue. Behind the mists of its apocalypses quite as much as in the Mishna, is this spring of Jewish life always to be seen, and complain though the people might of Pharisees who were but hypocrites, and of teachers who laid rather than removed burdens, they followed them by the thousands, if need be to death. The legalistic spirit had been too great an element in Jewish life, and its representatives — the Chasidim, the "Couples," the rabbis, the Pharisees, the Essenes — had furnished too many heroes, to be disregarded.

Of this more exacting religious life it is not possible to speak in detail. Its provisions are easily to be seen in the gospels, and to a far greater degree in the Talmud. For scrupulosity, unhesitating logic, conscientiousness as regards the moral aspect of every act in life it stands unparalleled. It is easy and even customary to see absurdity in talmudic discussions. Absurdity there may be, but a sympathetic reader will also feel that some determination as to the morality of every trivial detail is inevitable if righteousness is to be gained by obedience to any law. Thus in the case of the Sabbath, the minute grouping of all sorts of forbidden work into thirty-nine classes is no mere play of scholastic casuistry, but, if once the principle of legalism be granted, is a legitimate exposition of the distinction between permissible and forbidden actions. The great danger to which scribism yielded was that of moral pedantry and pride, but this was involved in legalism itself, and no one before Jesus felt the danger more keenly than the greater rabbis themselves. Despite its excesses, Pharisaism succeeded in grinding into the very soul of Jewish life, be it never so humble or degraded, moral distinctions as regards the acts of the individual, such as Hellenism even at its best never enforced.

When, however, all this and even more has been granted, it is abundantly clear that Pharisaism laid upon the people burdens impossible to be borne. The rabbis' insistence upon tithes and other religious charges must have been burdensome in the extreme, but even more deadening must have been their insistence that righteousness was impossible except through an unbroken observance of the Mosaic and the oral Law; for who among the people could hope to master the accumulation of rabbinical teaching? In proportion as legalism grew did the old prophetic teaching retreat, and life became less a direct service of a loving Jehovah and an ever increasingly fettered and hopeless succession, of impossible tasks.

Yet legalism could not kill the idealism that lay in the prophetical side of Jewish life. Whether learned or ignorant, gentle or fanatic, the Jew never lost his belief that the future held in store for his nation a universal empire, a kingdom of God. Other nations of antiquity had not been without ideals, but they had been either regretful recollections of a past Golden Age or philosophical and impossible Utopias like the republic of Plato. The Jew's hope was something other. His prophets spoke God's promises through God's inspiration. Frequently, it is true, idealists like Ezekiel and Zechariah had outlined reforms and a new Israel, and in nearly every case these reforms had been incorporated in the legislation of the times. Occasionally, also, the Pharisees had undertaken to improve irreligious institutions. But the hope for the Kingdom was not merely for a reformed Judea. The Kingdom was to be quite new and quite divine. God himself would establish it, and men had but to join it. Indeed, God was already king, with angels as subjects.

As something definitely expected, the kingdom of God was the slow outgrowth of the successive periods of misfortune which characterised the entire history of the Jewish people. Before the Persian period its faith had always looked to a regenerate Israel brought to greatness by Jehovah. Sometimes this faith grew specific, and saw with Isaiah and Jeremiah a miserably divided people reunited under the house of David, but oftener with Zephaniah, Habakkuk, Nahum, Obadiah, Joel, and Malachi, it dealt with national prosperity without naming the human king. The exile deepened the nation's consciousness of its peculiar relations with Jehovah, and with the return of the most devoted of its members there came a deepening of the hope that Israel would become a world power, directly ruled by God. But it was short-lived. The rise of the priestly class and of that practical spirit which finds expression in literature like Ecclesiastes and Ecclesiasticus, left little room for the idealism of faith. When, however, the misery of religious persecution awoke the Chasidim to a fuller realisation of their need of Jehovah and to a new prophetic era, the Kingdom became again an object of religious interest.

In this revival any hope of a specially appointed king — a Messiah — appeared but incidentally. Daniel's Son of Man was even less an individual than had been the Servant of Jehovah — nothing more than a type of the kingdom of the saints that should arise from the revolt against Syrian oppression. But shortly afterward there came also an increasing belief that none but an Anointed of God could lead the Jewish people into their great future. The authors of the earlier chapters in Enoch and the Sibyttine Oracles foresaw a man as well as a kingdom, and it has already appeared that the Pharisees, after their bitter disappointment at the course taken by the Asmonean house, still looked for the "Son of David," who should be "a just king taught of God." In this descent the two rival schools of Shammai and Hillel agreed. However they might differ as to the character of the Messiah, — whether, as the school of Shammai would say, he was to sweep away the Romans by the breath of his mouth, or, as the followers of Hillel believed, he was to be a prince of peace, — in either case he was to be from the branch of David. And of his kingdom of pious Jews there was to be no end.

In its essential elements this progressive conception was practically complete by the first century of our era. The rabbis were, it is true, to meet their Christian opponents and the fearful disillusions of history with new teachings, but they did little more than elaborate and supplement the older ideal with a suffering Messiah and a profusion of eschatological details. Thus, the Messianic hope, both as regards the kingdom and the Christ, was born of national misfortunes, and was cherished by those who dared to hope and trust Jehovah for a brighter future. It was no philosophy. It was a part of a national spirit, from the days of Alexandra growing more intense. Above all was it the possession of the Pharisees, the Essenes, and the Zealots. Yet it can hardly have been limited to them. The history of the Messianic movement begun by John, as well as the occurrences under the later procurators, make it clear that the masses also looked forward to a new and divine Jewish kingdom to be established by some one especially appointed (anointed) by God for the purpose. The Sadducees alone seem not to have shared in the hope.

It is naturally difficult to reproduce exactly and in detail this national expectation as it appeared among so many groups of men. The literature which has survived was probably that of but one or two schools of religionists, and the hope of the masses has to be reconstructed from incidental statements and allusions. Speaking generally, however, the hope took two expressions, — that of literature and that of popular feeling. In one thing, however, both agreed — the kingdom of God was to be a kingdom of Jews. All other people were to be its subjects or proselyted citizens. Of a kingdom in any other sense there is no trace, either in Pharisaic literature or in popular expectations, for whenever its subjects are said to be "the righteous" or "the sons of God," the context excludes a broader interpretation. But at this point divergence begins. There were those who expected some specially appointed hero, and others who apparently awaited no individual Messiah. Some expected the kingdom to be established politically in the world as they knew it; others in despair of earthly success awaited some fearful cataclysm that should presage a kingdom of risen saints.

The Messianic hope, as it appears in literature, is varied, if not inconsistent, in its details. If, however, we disregard all late rabbinical elements, it is possible to present it in its main outline. The advent of the kingdom of God was not only to be heralded by the return of Elijah, and possibly other prophets, but it was to be preceded by a period of fearful suffering, especially within Jerusalem. Nature itself would abound in awful portents, the moon and the sun turning to blood, the stars falling from their courses. The Messiah would suddenly appear whence no one knew, perhaps from Bethlehem, perhaps from Jerusalem, perhaps though this is probably a later conjecture from Rome. When he should come none knew, although the rabbis endeavoured to set the day by ingenious calculations. With the Messiah's coming would begin a last fierce war and judgment, in which the enemies of the Jews and all the evil angels would be destroyed, God himself being the judge.

With this judgment "this age" would end, and "the age to come" would begin. The new kingdom would be set up in Jerusalem, which itself would be renovated by the Messiah, if, indeed, a new Jerusalem did not descend from heaven. Peace would then spread over the world, the Dispersion would be recalled, and the righteous dead be raised from their graves to join the kingdom centred in, but by no means limited to, Palestine. God then would take over the kingdom, now as holy as glorious.

The character of the Messiah himself as expected by the Pharisees is somewhat indistinct, because of no attempt on their part to present it systematically.

With the Word of Alexandrine Stoicism and the Memra of rabbinism, the Messiah had little in common. He was, it will be recalled, rather an ideal king who should be God's agent in the establishment of his kingdom. This ideal was never so elaborated as to predicate divine qualities of the Messiah. Once or twice he was ascribed preexistence, but so far as the earlier rabbinism is concerned this was probably only ideal in the purpose of God, rather than personal. His titles, "Son of Man," and "Son of God," are seldom used, and his true character is to be seen in such titles as "King," "Anointed," "Son of David." He was, in fact, most likely thought of as a human king, especially chosen and fitted by God for establishing his kingdom, and as one who should after its consummation surrender it to his Lord.

If this be the literary and most refined Messianic hope, and especially if, as seems altogether probable, the hopes set forth in the Book of Enoch are those only of a narrow if not esoteric group, it is not difficult to imagine, even without the few hints of the gospels and Josephus, what the hope was among the masses. They, too, expected a new kingdom for Israel, but without waiting upon some conquest of righteousness. Repentance was but a means of escaping the punishment of the Judge. The Anointed of God would be no hero to overcome with "the word of his mouth," but a warrior under whose leadership the Jews would surely "tread upon the neck of the eagle." Rabbinical refinements, panaceas of eschatological visions, were thrust one side. The Christ would work miracles, but only when he had summoned Jews to arms.

It is precisely this aspect of the religious development of Judaism that offers the best point of view for understanding the movement inaugurated by Jesus of Nazareth. To discuss his work as a teacher of personal religion would carry us too far from our present study of the history of the Jews as a nation; but as a Jew transforming Judaism he cannot be overlooked. Like the Pharisees, Jesus found in the kingdom of God his highest ideal, but unlike them he deliberately refused to see in it anything political or ethnic; and while the Pharisees taught men to await it, Jesus urged men to join it as something already among them. Nor was it something outside the sphere of ethics. Far otherwise, it presupposed moral strenuousness, for one must strive to enter it. And, above all, he set himself forth as its founder — the Messiah.

It is very little that we know of Jesus outside his founding of the Messianic kingdom. He was a Galilean, though born in Bethlehem (6-5 B.C.). He was of Davidic descent, although he never appealed to this fact in the endeavour to win followers, and distinctly repudiated the rabbinical notions which had gathered about the term "Son of David." He learned his father's trade of carpentry and probably followed it until he began his public work. It is possible that before his public life he had won some local reputation as a pious and comparatively educated man, who, superficially judged, was in sympathy with Pharisaism of the less rigorous type. Of his inner life during these years of obscurity we can infer little except that he was an independent and profound student of the Hebrew Scriptures, a reader of other Jewish literature, and above all a man in a unique and utterly unparalleled degree at one with a God whom from his boyhood he knew as Father.

Both from his surroundings and his own nature, he must have been increasingly concerned with the kingdom of God. Yet the first steps in the actual Messianic movement which bears his name were not taken by him. In fact, up to the very beginning of his public career he appears to have had no suspicion that his sense of divine sonship would necessitate his abandonment of his quiet life in Nazareth. His awakening was occasioned by John the Baptist a product of the extreme ascetic religious spirit that always existed sporadically among the Jews, and altogether a different man from Jesus. In the garb of the poorest fellah John appeared suddenly among the effeminate inhabitants of the Jordan valley near Jericho, and gave his startling message. The day of Jehovah was at hand! The Christ was about to appear to sit in judgment upon all men! There was no time to be lost, and he summoned men and women to be bathed in the Jordan as evidence of their abandoning their sins in hopes of avoiding the punishment of the approaching Judge. His conceptions of the Kingdom differed from those of the Pharisees and Essenes, in that with him Jewish birth counted but little; but his words ran like wildfire among a people eager to believe that their hopes were to be fulfilled. Penitents came to him in crowds from Judea and Perea. As he worked northward the news of his work reached Nazareth, and Jesus, recognising in him a messenger of God, went to be baptized.

In the very water his duty burst upon him like a voice from God. He was to be the Messiah whom John, in ignorance, had foretold. He, and he alone, must found the kingdom of God.

In one way, the task was easy. He had but to accommodate himself to the hope of his people, win over Pharisee and populace by an appeal to national pride, organise a state. That such a plan would have succeeded is made almost certain by the subsequent career of Mohamet in almost the same region and among a people inferior to the Jews. But over against this current ideal of the kingdom lay the ideal of Jesus himself: of a new social order, in which God should reign, and men should do his will; in which men should be sons of God, and, therefore, brothers of each other. And he chose to establish this ethical and religious fraternity, though he saw that the attempt, so similar to those of the prophets of his race, would almost certainly bring him to their fate. Over against conquest and world-wide supremacy he chose love and self-sacrifice.

His method was at once simple and farsighted. From the start, the movement was Messianic, but Jesus was more concerned to show that the Messiah was such as he, than to show that he was the Messiah. In other words, like a prophet, rather than a rabbi, he used current hopes in the service of ethics and religion. His effort was also social. Thanks to John, who believed him to be the Christ, Jesus immediately found himself the centre of a little group of common people — 'am haarets — who accepted him as the Christ of popular expectation. Perhaps because of this fact, the first few months of the new movement were filled with work similar to that of John, and men were summoned to repentance and baptism. These months were spent in Judea, but proximity to John exposed each Messianic movement to danger and Jesus returned to Galilee. There, when John had been imprisoned, he began his great work of evangelisation, philanthropy, and the education of his closest friends, and it is of his life among the Galileans that we know most from the gospels.

Of his teaching during these months, we cannot speak. It is enough to say that, as the founder of the kingdom of God, he did not commit himself to either Pharisaic or popular Messianic hopes. For a considerable time he was less interested in being accepted as the Messiah than in showing men the requisites of membership in the Messianic kingdom. He seldom, if ever, used the term "Christ" with reference to himself, and commonly spoke of himself as "the Son of Man," which, though Messianic in of Enoch, apparently had little or no such content in the thoughts of the people at large. For this very reason, it was a most serviceable term. In its original force in Daniel it presented a man as the type of a "kingdom of the saints," as beasts were the types of other kingdoms. By using it, Jesus could clearly and without precipitating any disturbance, set forth a distinct ideal of membership in the kingdom of God, for the word would suggest to every Jew the simple typology of Daniel, and Jesus would thus stand as the type of the kingdom he announced. His character should be that of its members. For, as the Messiah, he was something more than a teacher — he was a Life. It was his consciousness of divine sonship that had led him to undertake the Messianic work of establishing God's kingdom, and it was the same consciousness that gave him his power of inspiring a few men with an undying loyalty to himself. As a teacher of ethics, he could do little more than restate, though with astonishing simplicity and force, the great principles already taught by the Hebrew prophets; but as the Messiah, he founded the kingdom of God, by compelling men who could not understand him or his ideals to love him, and grow to be like him, the ideal of the kingdom.

From the beginning of his preaching in Galilee, Jesus was a popular hero. His sweetness of temper, the authority and attractiveness in his teaching, his undisguised sympathy with the despised masses, his superiority to his religious superiors, his philanthropy, the very mystery in his Messianic character — all brought thousands to him. But he did not exploit his popularity. He once retired to the hills when the crowds were on the point of making him a leader of revolution, and repeatedly he endeavoured to escape their presence. Nor did he attempt to win everybody to himself. In his teachings he seems occasionally to magnify difficulties that he might dissuade any half-hearted person from joining the group of his immediate friends.

To the members of this never very numerous, though by no means small, circle he showed his ideals as rapidly as they could appreciate them, and thus developed their better natures without destroying prematurely their old beliefs. By degrees one thing grew true of them all — they grew less devoted to Pharisaic supremacy. Jesus, it is true, was always loyal to the pre-Pharisaic faith of his people, the temple and its services, the Law in its broader teachings, and even to professional teachers. But with Pharisaism as a system he broke entirely. To him righteousness was an affair of motive and inner character, and religion as he knew it and lived it was not a keeping of traditional laws, but a life with God, and his opposition to the heartless pedantry that so often was the ideal of Pharisaism grew intense. By degrees his disciples came to take the same position, and almost before they could appreciate it, the Pharisees found themselves confronting a popular movement, which, if successful, would end fasting as a religious duty, make the Sabbath observance vastly less strict, abolish the distinction between clean and unclean things altogether, make stricter all teachings as to marriage and divorce, lessen the influence of the oral Law, give new importance to the masses and less to the professional classes, destroy the ultra-national character of the expected kingdom, — a movement which, in a word, would undo most of the political and social development which had made them the popular leaders. That a struggle should have ensued was inevitable. The very foundations of society seemed threatened.

The attack came from the rabbis of Jerusalem, and was not upon the new fraternity, but upon Jesus himself. It passed rapidly through the several stages of suspicion, hatred, and conspiracy. As long as Jesus was in Galilee, it is true, his popularity among the 'am haarets, as well as the distance from Jerusalem, kept his opponents from inflicting upon him the punishment due to heretics, but they hindered his public work in the country, and at last forced him to leave Galilee altogether.

Before they succeeded even this far, however, Jesus had a few months — or rather, perhaps, weeks — in which he conducted an indefatigable canvass of Galilee. His kingdom was not to be an institution, but a fraternity, as broad as human life. Choosing twelve men from the many who believed in him, — a belief that was only imperfect in his Messiahship, but complete in his ability to teach truth and work cures, — he sent them out to announce the coming kingdom to villages he could not himself visit. But their efforts were apparently not often repeated, and he preferred to keep them with him that their ideas as to him and his fraternity might be clarified.

When at last he was forced to leave Galilee these men went with him, first into the neighbouring regions of Tyre and Sidon, then into the heathen Decapolis, and finally into Perea and Judea. It was at the beginning of these few months of wanderings, half as fugitives and half as teachers, that Jesus brought his twelve followers to see clearly that despite all the opposition of the Pharisees and the startling differences between his life and their own expectations, he was yet the Christ. From the moment of their confession of a faith which if incomplete was larger and more intelligent than when they had first joined him, he unfolded to them the suffering he saw must be the outcome of the opposition of their religious leaders, and for which as a final test their faith must be prepared. He himself did not waver in either purpose or teaching, and when in the spring of 29 he and the twelve other young men went up to the Passover, it was with the purpose of publicly announcing himself as the Christ. With this end in view, during the last few days in his life, he performed a number of acts expected of the Messiah. Thus, he rode into the city on an ass, accepting the shouts of those who hailed him as the Son of David; he cleansed the temple; he defined Messiahship. But all was in vain. His very popularity, which suddenly blazed up as if in Galilee itself, increased his danger. So far from being only an heretical Galilean lay preacher, he appeared an incipient, if not an open, revolutionist. His persistent effort to be understood as unpolitical was overlooked. The Sadducees joined with the Pharisees in planning to put him out of the way. It was better, the high priest said, that one man should die than that the nation should perish. Jesus knew his danger, but still lingered in Jerusalem to eat the Passover of his people, and, if possible, win over the crowds of religionists to his conception of the real kingdom of God. For he saw clearly to what political death the popular conception would lead the nation. Secure in his belief that his Father yet had work for him to do, and protected by the presence of his Galilean friends, he went openly about the capital, and openly attacked the Pharisees and rabbis because of their elevation of the unimportant over the essential elements of religion. Yet it is probable he would have returned to Galilee in safety had he not been betrayed by one of the twelve. During the night after the Passover he was suddenly arrested. Early the next morning he was tried and condemned at an irregular meeting of the Sanhedrin. The Sadducean priests were especially insistent, and finally the procurator, Pontius Pilate, was induced to approve the sentence as a political necessity. Jesus was crucified as a revolutionist — the "King of the Jews," and buried before night.

Had he been simply a teacher, the story would probably have to stop here. But he had done more than teach — he had founded the kingdom of God, and its members, then in Jerusalem, though few in number, remained together, and not being molested by the city officials, waited, they knew not what. And then on the Sunday after the Friday on which Jesus had been buried began a series of experiences, which, were they not well attested, it would be impossible to believe. For not one or two, but many — even hundreds — maintained they saw Jesus again, no longer dead, but living gloriously, "the first fruits of those who slept."

Then, better than before, though still but incompletely, did they appreciate the significance of his life and death as parts of his Messianic work, and, after a few weeks spent at Jerusalem, they began the task of converting their nation. But Jesus was no longer the humble, neglected teacher. He was a man anointed of God with the Holy Ghost, and shown to be the Christ by having been raised from the dead. But at once the influence of their old Messianic hopes was felt. Jesus himself during the last days of his life had made some use of the eschatological elements of the older hope, and these the disciples now seized upon almost to the exclusion of all else. The kingdom had not yet come, but would appear suddenly. Jesus was, indeed, the Messiah; but his proper Messianic work would not begin until his second coming, this time in glory in the clouds of heaven. The group of disciples, now growing rapidly, no longer was thought of as a kingdom that, however small, would yet, like leaven, transform all society; but as a congregation, a community of men and women engaged in preparing themselves by a holy life to welcome their Lord at his appearing, and then to reign with him in glory indescribable.

And thus out of a Judaism, at once legalistic and idealistic, there sprang a movement which, though not abandoning either Mosaism or Pharisaism, supplemented both by a passionate belief that the Messiah had appeared, that the preparation for his final coming in judgment was moral and ethical, and that the great Messianic kingdom was at any moment to be established by the very Jesus whom the Jews had in their ignorance crucified. From the day of Jesus, the Jewish people were thus to cherish two ideals of the kingdom of God that of the Pharisee and Zealot and that of the Christian. Each ideal had its future, but so far as we know, Jesus was the one person who foresaw what these futures would be. His lamentations over the cities of Galilee and Jerusalem were prophecies of the inevitable outcome of the rejection of the future he might have given Judea, as certainly as, through his followers, he has made Christian people the arbiters of the world. For the Messianism of Pharisee and Zealot was to bring the Jewish nation to its end.

CHAPTER XIV: HEROD AGRIPPA I AND HEROD AGRIPPA II

THE early years of Christianity had little or no influence upon Judaism. The community of those who accepted Jesus as the Messiah, the church, remained loyal to the temple and the synagogue, and was in fact a sect of the Jews. But before any considerable time had passed there sprang up within the church a new group headed by Stephen, one of seven men chosen to relieve the twelve of a part of their rapidly increasing work. This group saw that if Jesus really were the Christ, Judaism was no longer final, and with this conviction its members attacked the exclusiveness of Pharisasm in much the same spirit as Jesus himself. As might have been expected, Judaism was enraged. Stephen met his Master's fate, and there broke out a fierce attack upon the new sect. This persecution, however, but intensified the Christians' zeal, and wherever they were scattered they organised new communities. The persecution was doubtless Sadducean in part, but its chief agent was a Pharisee, Saul of Tarsus. In him religious persecution had its most conscientious agent, and Judaism its most consistent representative. Yet when the persecution was at its height Saul himself was converted, and immediately took Stephen's position more distinctly than had Stephen himself. Although his first work is not clearly recorded, it seems that from the moment of his conversion he saw that others than Jews would share in the Messianic kingdom, and that therefore the good news should be preached to them. His work as a result lay outside of Palestine, and the churches of Jerusalem and Judea remained Jewish, the mass of their members as devoted to the oral Law as before their acceptance of Jesus as the Christ. None the less, the religious authorities of Judea seem to have been suspicious of them, even if persecution for a time was stilled.

While thus the new fraternity was spreading in all directions, the history of Palestinian Judaism developed along the lines already set by Pharisaism. The administration of Pilate was brought to a close by events that very well represent the power of the rabbis. As if in imitation of Jesus, there appeared a prophet in Samaria who promised to reveal the hiding place of the sacred vessels Moses was believed to have buried on Mount Gerizim.

The Samaritans assembled in large numbers in answer to his call, all with arms. Pilate, fearing a revolt, attacked the gathering, killing and imprisoning many of the crowd. Thereupon the Samaritans complained to Vitellius, then on a special mission to Syria, and by him Pilate was compelled to go to Rome for trial, Marcellus being made procurator in his stead.

The downfall of Pilate is only one evidence of the more friendly attitude of Rome toward Judea that characterised the later years of Tiberius. Even before this event Pilate had been obliged by the emperor, in answer to the urgent petition of the sons of Herod, to take down some votive shields he had hung up in the royal palace at Jerusalem. Vitellius now apparently attempted still further to conciliate the Jews. He attended the Passover at Jerusalem, where he remitted taxes upon the sale of fruit, and gave up the high priests' robes, which, since the beginning of the procuratorial administration, partly because of an ancient custom, partly as a sort of pledge of good conduct, had been honourably kept by the Romans in the castle of Antonia. He still kept control of the appointment of high priests, however, but probably used it also in such a way as to please the people. A further act of conciliation was shown, when, in his expedition against Petra, he inarched through Esdraelon and Perea, rather than carry his standards through Judea.

The death of Tiberius enabled Caligula to do Pharisaism an even greater service by appointing Herod Agrippa, son of Aristobulus, and grandson of Herod I, as king over what had been the tetrarchy of Philip as well as the small tetrarchy of Lysanias (37 A.D.).

The account of this man's life reads like a romance. Educated, like the other Herodian princes, in Rome, he had there acquired the habits of the early empire, and at the age of forty found himself in disfavour with Tiberius, bankrupt, and a fugitive from his creditors. He succeeded in reaching Palestine, where he shut himself up in a tower on the border of the southern desert, and would have committed suicide had it not been for his energetic wife, Cypros. As a last resort she went to Agrippa's sister, Herodias, who had already married Herod Antipas, and through her obtained from the tetrarch the appointment of Agrippa as superintendent of markets in Tiberias. Such a humiliating position could not long satisfy the man, and, because of a quarrel over their cups, Agrippa left his uncle-brother-in-law to get aid from his friend Flaccus, the propraetor of Syria. With him he remained until his brother, Aristobulus, detecting him accepting bribes from the citizens of Damascus, reported him to Flaccus, who forced the unhappy man again out upon his wanderings. Reduced to the last extremities, Agrippa determined to go once more to Italy. With the aid of his freedman, Maesgas, he succeeded in borrowing a considerable sum of money and started for Egypt, barely escaping arrest for debt as he was leaving Anthedon. At Alexandria he borrowed a much larger sum from the brother of Philo on his wife's credit, and thus equipped, sent his family back to Judea, while he went on to Rome. There he became intimate with Caius, who, with all the empire, was waiting impatiently for Tiberius to die. Unfortunately Agrippa expressed this desire before a charioteer who, in revenge for some injury, repeated it to the old emperor, and Agrippa was promptly thrown into chains. He was not released until Caius was finally seated as emperor. Once appointed king he seems to have spent much of his time in Rome, where his friendship with the emperor won him also the territories of the unlucky Herod Antipas (39 A.D.), and enabled him to render the Jews service at an important crisis.

The accession of the mad Caligula was an occasion for a new outburst of anti-semitism, and Agrippa was unintentionally its occasion. For his presence in Alexandria was made the occasion for a considerable outbreak against the Jews, who would not join with the other provincials in paying divine honours to the emperor. The Jewish quarter was pillaged, men and women abused, and statues of Caligula were placed in the synagogues. The governor of Alexandria had even taken from the Jews the rights of citizenship in the city. The outbreak finally became a genuine persecution, and the Jews appealed to the emperor. But their embassy, although headed by Philo himself, accomplished nothing; for Caligula, instead of listening to their petition, asked them why they would not eat pork! At the same time, the monomania of Caligula as to his divinity, brought even more serious difficulties upon Judea itself. The heathen citizens of Jamnia erected an altar to the emperor, and the Jewish citizens immediately destroyed it. The deed was reported to the emperor, and immediately he gave orders to have his statue erected in the temple at Jerusalem, and Petronius, the legate of Syria, was sent with a strong force to see that the command was fulfilled. The Jews were overwhelmed with despair, and begged Petronius to kill them rather than do their temple the indignity. Fortunately, the legate was a considerate man, and at the request of Agrippa and other prominent Jews in various ways delayed the fulfilment of the order until he had personally appealed to Caligula. Agrippa was himself in Rome when the legate's letter arrived, and was able, at a banquet, to win from the emperor a reversal of the command. Petronius, however, was directed to commit suicide, but escaped his fate through the assassination of the emperor.

With the accession of Claudius (41 A.D.), a new era seemed to open for the Jews. Singularly enough, Claudius was under considerable obligation to Agrippa for his elevation to the empire, and promptly met it by giving him all the territory that had belonged to Herod I, together with the right to appoint the high priests. In addition, he gave Agrippa's brother, Herod, the little kingdom of Chalcis, returned to the Jews of Alexandria their old privileges, and extended equal rights to Jews throughout the empire (41 A.D.).

This revival of the kingdom of Judea, under an Asmonean-Herodian, gave a new impulse to Judaism. Far more than his grandfather, Agrippa, though by no means unfriendly to Hellenism, was regardful of his subjects' religious convictions. From the first he observed the customs and ceremonies enforced by Pharisaism; lived in Jerusalem; kept all portraits off the coinage of Jerusalem; guarded the sanctity of Jewish synagogues, even in Phoenicia; appointed an acceptable high priest; compelled a prospective son-in-law to be circumcised; and himself took part in the services of the temple, where he was saluted by the people as their true brother. He also attacked Christianity, killing James and arresting Peter. There are even indications that he had ambitions to build up Judea into the head of a confederacy of allied kingdoms, for he strengthened the fortifications of Jerusalem greatly, and would undoubtedly have made the city impregnable had Claudius not commanded him to stop the work. He also held a conference of five kings at Tiberias, although this was broken up by the legate of Syria before it had accomplished anything.

Yet, while thus careful to maintain the best relations with his people, Agrippa was enough of a Herodian to be fond of the amusements of the Graeco-Roman world. One of his coins, struck by Gaza, represents a temple of Marna, and at Berytus (Beirut) he built baths, colonnades, a theatre, and an amphitheatre, at the opening of which fourteen hundred criminals were made to slaughter each other. He also celebrated games at Caesarea, in honour of the emperor. It was, in fact, at these games that he was suddenly struck down by a mysterious and fatal disease, just as he had allowed his courtiers to address him as a god (44 A.D.).

With his death the second short halcyon age of Judaism closed. It had been the first intention of Claudius to make Agrippa II, the only son of Agrippa I, then a boy of seventeen years, king in his father's place; but his court had persuaded him to do otherwise, and for a short time the entire kingdom of Judea was under a procurator. Agrippa, however, was soon to enjoy something of the good fortune that belonged to his house. The procurator, Fadus, though clearing Judea of robbers, had marked the return of a Roman administration by seizing the vestment of the high priest, and putting it again into the castle of Antonia, where it might be under his control, as it had been under that of the earlier procurators. The Jews bitterly resented the act, and with the consent of Fadus, and Longinus, the propraetor of Syria, they sent an embassy to Claudius, asking that the vestments be left in their own keeping. Agrippa lent his influence to the petition, and was able to gain a favourable decision from the emperor. As a further proof of his regard, Claudius gave Agrippa, in the eighth year of his reign (49-50 A.D.), the kingdom of Chalcis, which had belonged to his uncle, Herod. With this little kingdom went the authority over the temple and the sacred money, as well as the right to appoint the high priest, all of which Herod had obtained from Claudius. About this time Agrippa was again of great service to the Jews in bringing about the acquittal of the high priest Ananias, and Ananus the commander of Jerusalem, both of whom Cumanus had sent to the imperial court, under the charge of fomenting rebellion. In 53 A.D. he exchanged the kingdom of Chalcis for the tetrarchy of Philip, to which were added, by Nero, portions of Perea and Galilee, including, among others, the city of Tiberias. A much weaker man than his father, Agrippa II maintained friendships with Pharisee and heathen alike, but succeeded in winning considerable favour from the rabbis themselves. Yet his long reign (50-100) resulted in nothing of importance, and when the Jew and Roman were at last at war, Agrippa II was found fighting against his countryman.

CHAPTER XV: THE FALL Of JUDEA AND THE RISE OF THE CHRISTIAN CHURCH

WITH the death of Agrippa I there began a series of procurators who, with the exception of Fadus, were worthy representatives in Judea of emperors like Claudius and Nero in Rome. Yet under Fadus, Judaism seemed to enjoy nearly the same privileges as under Agrippa I, for although he attempted at first to control the vestments of the high priest, he readily allowed the matter to be adjudicated. During his administration, also, Queen Helena, of Adiabene, visited the city, sent it provisions in time of famine, and finally was buried just outside its walls. But under him began the succession of disturbances that led directly to the great outbreak in 66 A.D. The nation was filled with Messianic hopes and at one time a certain Theudas promised to divide the Jordan and to lead his followers across it to some unknown blessings. Fadus dispersed the crowd and beheaded Theudas, but brought no quiet to the country. Under Alexander, the next procurator, who, though a nephew of Philo, had abandoned Judaism, the two sons of that Judas of Galilee who had led the revolt at the time of the taxing under Quirinius, were crucified, probably for some attempt at insurrection. Under Cumanus a terrible massacre of Jews took place at the Passover, as a punishment for their rioting, because of a soldier's indecent insult to the temple. Another riot, due to another soldier's abuse of some sacred books, was prevented only by the execution of the offender. At another time, as the Galileans were going up to the Passover through Samaria, they were attacked near Ginea (Jeniri) by the Samaritans. As Cumanus had been bribed not to punish the offenders, a body of Jews under Eleazar and Alexander, two "robbers," burned several Samaritan villages and killed their inhabitants. Cumanus, in turn, fell upon the invaders, killing some and imprisoning others. The matter was then carried to Quadratus, legate of Syria, and by him to Claudius. Thanks to the influence of Agrippa II the Jews won their case, and Cumanus was banished; Felix, the brother of the notorious Pallas, being sent as procurator in his stead.

Under Felix the rebellious elements of Jewish life became even more evident, and the country was disturbed by Zealots and impostors who persuaded crowds to follow them into the wilderness where they promised to work signs by the power of God. How far these men represented some turbulent Messianism it is not possible to say, but doubtless to a considerable extent. One prophet in particular, an Egyptian, seems to have posed as a sort of Messiah, for he gathered a great crowd upon the Mount of Olives, promising to make the walls of Jerusalem fall. Felix scattered the mob, but the Egyptian himself escaped. The disturbances, however, were repeated, and Felix was constantly compelled to disperse crowds of men, "clean in their hands," who were looking for divine deliverance. In addition there were the bands of "robbers," in whom, because of their popularity, it is easy to see revolutionists rather than mere bandits. One of their leaders, Eleazar, maintained himself for twenty years. Felix captured great numbers of these men, crucifying some and sending others to Rome, but was unable to destroy the movement. Instead, the feeling of the people grew the more intense. Bands of Zealots ranged through the country, urging men to revolt, plundering the well-to-do citizens, killing and burning. At the same time bands of Sicarii — men who carried daggers under their clothes — began an almost systematic assassination of their enemies, beginning with the high priest, whose death was also desired by the procurator himself.

Had Felix been a strong governor or a good man, this incipient anarchy might have been checked, but he lost the respect of his subjects as much by the laxity of his life as by the bursts of severity with which he punished all offenders. The country grew full of unrest and violence, of high priests quarrelling with the lower priests, or Jews quarrelling with heathen, of humble people eager to join in a revolt, and when Felix was recalled by Nero, he left a country which though legally enjoying exceptional privileges, had been excited by its fanatical citizens into incipient rebellion (60-61 A.D.).

The successor of Felix was Porcius Festus [60(61)-62], a man of good intentions, but whose untimely death forbade his short administration's leaving any permanent good effects. Like Felix, he was compelled to deal with the Sicarii and with an impostor who promised his followers deliverance from their miseries if they would but follow him into the wilderness.

Both Felix and Festus are of especial interest from the fact that Paul — the Saul of earlier days — was brought before them on charges preferred by the authorities of Jerusalem. He had been arrested in the temple on the false charge of having brought Gentiles beyond their court; had been nearly killed by the mob, and nearly tortured by the Roman centurion as one of the numerous impostors. After a trial before the Sanhedrin, he had been sent down to Caesarea to protect him from a band of Sicarii who had vowed to kill him. Neither Felix nor Festus could find any ground on which to keep him in prison, beyond the general hostility of the Jews and the possibility that he might be another agitator. Festus proposed to take him up to Jerusalem again for trial, but Paul appealed to Caesar and accordingly was sent to Rome shortly after the arrival of Festus. It is noteworthy that beyond the case of Paul, the Christians do not seem to have attracted the attention of the procurators.

The successor of Festus was one Albinus (62-64), but he did not reach Judea until several months after the death of Festus. During this interregnum, the high priest Ananus, the second of the name, a noble man and a persistent enemy of Zealotry, to which he at last fell a victim, undertook to clear the country of dangerous characters. He therefore seized James the brother of Jesus, and after having had him tried by the Sanhedrin, caused him to be stoned. Agrippa, however, deposed Ananus after a pontificate of only three months, and the national unrest was left without an enemy. While the Pharisees were ready to abide by their legal rights, the anti-Roman feeling grew more intense among the Zealots. The Sicarii constantly kidnapped the servants of the high priest in order to compel their master to bring about by exchange the release of some of their own number then in prison, and not content with this ravaged the whole country. Rival high priests engaged in miniature civil war. Desperate members of the nobility turned robbers, and to cap all, Albinus, who seems to have received bribes by the wholesale, in order to gain favour with the Jews when once he learned he was to be removed, sold their freedom to all Jews who had been imprisoned on trifling charges, killed the others, and left the jails empty. And in the midst of all this disorder we find Levites petitioning Agrippa to let them wear the robes of priests, and Agrippa permitting the priests to use the temple treasures to pave the entire city with white stone and thus give employment to eighteen thousand workmen left idle by the (64 A.D.) completion of the temple.

The last procurator was Gessius Florus, who, according to Josephus, so outdid Albinus in wickedness, that in comparison that rascal seemed a benefactor. He is said to have robbed cities and to have become a partner with highwaymen. He devastated whole toparchies, mocked his subjects' complaints to Cestius Gallus, legate of Syria, and in order to prevent complaints reaching the emperor; endeavoured to drive the Jews into open rebellion. But these charges are so indefinite as to raise suspicion. In fact, most of the accusations brought by Josephus against the procurators, when thoroughly sifted, witness to their desire to maintain order by punishing murderers and agitators rather than to wickedness. Doubtless they did fail to sympathise with all the prejudices of the Jews, and they were certainly open to bribes; but their bad administration might, like that of Felix, have been brought to punishment at the imperial court. The real destroyers of the Jewish state, as Jesus had foretold and as Josephus himself at times sees, were the Zealot Messianic party with its following among the poorer classes. They deliberately sought to found a kingdom of God upon earth with the dagger and the sword. And they had their wish.

Under Floras, the revolutionary movement got control of Jerusalem, and so of Judea, through a succession of events that were thoroughly trivial. A quarrel in Caesarea over buildings crowding in upon a synagogue, a series of petty insults added to the old causes of hatred between Jews and Greeks in that city, a mistake of Florus, an impudent jest against the procurator — these it was that precipitated as desperate and murderous a war as the world has seen. It is needless to recall the details fully. It is enough to say that when Florus had gone to Jerusalem instead of to Caesarea, despite the prayers of Berenice, sister of Agrippa II, then in Jerusalem fulfilling a vow, he allowed his soldiers to plunder the city and even to kill many of its inhabitants as a punishment. For a moment it looked as if Agrippa and the well-to-do classes would be able to persuade the masses to follow the legal course of complaint to the emperor, and to pay their taxes already due; but when it came to submitting again to Florus, the people would not listen, and broke out into new violence. A band of Sicarii captured Masada, and other revolutionists seized the lower city and the temple, shutting up the more aristocratic classes in the upper city, and engaged in desultory battles with such forces as were at hand to maintain the peace. The long-standing hatred between social classes helped to swell the madness. The Sicarii joined the crowds in the lower city, attacked and burned the palaces of the high priest, Agrippa, and Berenice, and then set fire to the public archives and all bonds in order to cancel all debts. In the meantime a Galilean, Manahem, another son of Judas, forced the garrison to flee from Antonia, killed the high priest Ananias, and set himself up as king. But he was not the sort of Messiah wanted, and the Zealots under Eleazar captured him, and, after torturing, killed him. The breach with Rome was completed by the priests' ceasing to offer sacrifices for the emperor and by the slaughter of the Roman garrison who had surrendered.

As in France after the capture of the Bastile, the news of these events threw all Syria into disorder. Palestine was filled with wandering bands of Jews, who sacked and burned many of the Graeco-Roman cities, or their dependent towns, while others of these cities — and Alexandria as well — massacred the Jews living within them. At this juncture Cestius Gallus, the Syrian legate, undertook to restore peace. Dividing his forces, he sent one army to capture Joppa and its neighbourhood, while the other reduced Galilee. Both objects were accomplished without great difficulty, and he then marched upon Jerusalem, driving the few Jewish troops before him. At Gabao (el Jeb), a few miles from the capital, he was attacked fiercely, but unsuccessfully, and then, unwilling to appeal to force, endeavoured to persuade the Jews to surrender by the appeals of Agrippa. In this he was thwarted by the murderous patriotism of the Zealots. Then, perhaps seeing the impossibility of taking the city, he retired. The Jews followed him, hanging upon his rear and flanks, and at last attacked him in the narrow valley of Beth-horon, nearly annihilating his entire army. Cestius saved himself and a fraction of his forces, only by precipitate flight to Antioch. All his artillery, together with most of his baggage and large quantities of weapons, fell into the hands of the Jews, most of the treasure going to Eleazar the Zealot.

With this victory a new stage began in the revolt, for the well-to-do and official classes, seeing war to be inevitable, undertook to organise the state upon a revolutionary basis. Although many prominent citizens left Jerusalem at this time, enough remained to begin the organisation of the state upon Pharisaic lines. If the Messiah had not come, Judea should at least be a nation; and the subsequent history of this period (66-70 A.D.) may very well be viewed as a political experiment on the part of the moderate, and then of the fanatical devotees to Messianism. At the outset, of the two parties, the more radical, with Eleazar, the treasurer of the temple, at its head, was not represented in the government. Although the people of Jerusalem conducted the revolt, the Sanhedrin was undoubtedly in control of affairs, and its appointees were from the party of aristocratic, moderate revolutionists. At the head of this moderate party — whose purpose, undoubtedly, was to treat as soon as possible with the Romans — stood Ananus, the former high priest. A number of prominent men were chosen to organise the revolt throughout the country, and to take the first steps in the establishment of the old aristocratic republic of pre-Asmonean days, though apparently with a high priest deprived of political powers.

Probably the most important of the fields thus allotted to these "deputies on mission" was Galilee, certain to be the first point of the Roman attack, and Galilee was given to the young and clever, but thoroughly inexperienced, Josephus, the future historian. His position was by no means a sinecure. The Galileans were divided into two parties: one of which, composed of Greeks, and, doubtless, the great mass of the Jews, had no desire to become involved in a war with Rome; while the other was composed of as fanatical Zealots as were to be found in Judea itself. With the first party, Josephus succeeded very well. Doubtless, they shared in his general policy of carrying resistance just far enough to forestall the Zealots, and to win favourable terms from Rome. But, with those possessed of downright determination to fight to the death; with the fanatics who destroyed the palace of Herod Antipas at Tiberias because of its sculptures; and especially with one John of Gischala, the leader of a band of four hundred desperate patriots with such men, Josephus had the greatest difficulty. While he was bustling about the country, building walls, organising his raw levies as best he knew after the Roman fashion, haranguing them in the cause of discipline and moderation, forcing his troops to return stolen goods, and organising a revolutionary government, with its central council of seventy and its local councils of seven, John was imploring the Sanhedrin to remove the half-hearted doctrinaire, and, when that effort failed, was endeavouring to assassinate him. Many and great were the dangers to which the shifty Josephus was exposed; but, by infinite strategy, he delivered himself out of them all — to live to write of his experiences with such delightful self-appreciation that, despite its horrors, his story of the war in Galilee almost serves as a serio-comic introduction to the fearful tragedy enacted, three years later, at Jerusalem.

When Vespasian finally marched against Galilee, most of the work of Josephus went to the limbo of all paper republics. Sepphoris, the most powerful city in Galilee, opened its gates to the invaders, and the revolutionary army with its captains of thousands and hundreds and tens fled to the mountain strongholds. The war in Galilee thus became simply the process of capturing these strongholds. Jotapata, in which Josephus himself had taken refuge, fell after a siege full of desperate adventures, and Josephus was taken prisoner, but only to be treated with honour by

Vespasian because of his prophecy as to the victor's future. Gadara, Joppa, Tiberias, fell into Vespasian's hands. Tarichaea, a city a little south of Tiberias, was taken after a bloody naval battle upon the Sea of Galilee and its citizens slaughtered, sold into slavery, or sent to Greece to help dig Nero's canal across the isthmus of Corinth. The Samaritans were slaughtered on Mount Gerizim, and by September all Galilee and the other rebellious regions north of Judea were subdued with the exception of Gamala in Gaulanitis, Mount Tabor, and Gischala (el-Jish). Gamala alone offered any resistance, but fell after a heroic defence. Vespasian systematically completed the isolation of Jerusalem by the capture of all outlying cities of importance, and in each case the history of Galilee was repeated. The mass of people submitted readily to the Romans, while the bands of Zealots, like John of Gischala, retreated to Jerusalem, there to swell the already crowded population.

But with these successes of the Romans came a new phase in the history of the revolt. Vespasian had begun the second year's campaign with vigour, but had hardly completed the subjection of the outlying cities of Judea (68), when news of the death of Nero caused him to suspend hostilities and await events. The Jews, thus relieved from immediate danger, at once came under the influence of the radical revolutionary party in Jerusalem. The fall of Galilee had showed the inefficiency of the aristocratic revolution, and with the arrival of John of Gischala, who had escaped from his city just before it fell, Jerusalem was divided between the two parties — the Zealots, with Eleazar and John at their head, and the moderates led by Ananus and other prominent priests and rabbis. In a way, the struggle is thus seen to be a rising of the poor against the rich, as well as against Rome. At first the moderate party was successful, and shut their opponents up in the temple, where, in fact, they might have been destroyed but for the regard in which the temple was held. As it was, Anarius set a guard around the sacred enclosure, and kept the Zealots close prisoners. The moderate party was at the point of victory, when, at the suggestion of John, the Zealots induced a band of fanatical Idumeans to come to their aid by the plea that Ananus and his party were tyrants. During a great storm these "men from Marseilles" were admitted into the city, and instantly inaugurated a reign of terror. Ananus and all prominent members of the moderate party were slaughtered mercilessly. For days robbery and murder held high carnival in the name of liberty and the kingdom of God, until, at last, the Idumeans, convinced that they had been deceived by the Zealots, sickened of their work, released such prisoners as lived, and left the city, leaving John of Gischala in control of the revolution. The revolt had become anti-aristocratic, as well as anti-Roman, and the old hatred of the Sadducees and the rich now was unchecked. A certain Simon ben-Giora — Simon, the son of the Proselyte — gathered a band of desperate malcontents, and succeeded in getting control of much of the region east of Jordan, and of Idumea, including Hebron. The Zealots, still bent upon an orderly republic, attempted to check him, and had at one time captured his wife, but Simon soon brought them to terms. In the meantime, perhaps from his desire to prepare for the struggle with Rome, to which no one else in Jerusalem seems to have given any thought, John seems to have governed somewhat tyrannically, and the remnants of the old moderate party, together with many disaffected Zealots, brought Simon into the city as an ally. Immediately a new reign of terror was begun, and the crowds of Jews within the walls were exposed to new miseries. So far from Simon's reducing John, there were now in Jerusalem three hostile revolutionary armies: the Galilean Zealots under John, encamped upon the Temple Mount; the other Zealots who held the inner court of the temple — in itself a formidable fortress; and the wild men of Simon ben-Giora, who held the upper city, and indeed practically the rest of Jerusalem. These three bands — by no means to be confused with the wretched inhabitants of the city themselves — soon engaged in a mad war of mutual destruction. Although neither party interfered in the sacrifices in the temple, all the places about the temple were destroyed, the sacred timbers used for engines of war, the city itself became half desert and half camp, and almost all of the grain in the city was burnt.

All this misery lasted throughout 69 A.D., when Vespasian was fighting for possession of the empire; and even when Titus appeared before the city just before the Passover of 70 A.D., he found the city still less intent upon defence than upon the issues of civil war. Titus was actually before the gates of the city when John of Gischala, taking advantage of the crowds at the feast, smuggled some of his men into the inner court of the temple and assassinated Eleazar. With the rival parties thus reduced to two, union was somewhat easier, and thereafter John and Simon laboured together in the defence of the city.

Jerusalem was impregnable on all sides but the north. There, the wall begun by Agrippa I, and completed by the Jews just as the Romans appeared, surrounded the suburb of Bezetha. Within it ran the second wall from east to west, and within this lay the great castle-like temple flanked by the Tower of Antonia and separated from the city by a series of walls, while upon the higher western hill lay the upper city, protected by its own massive fortifications. Jerusalem was in fact a cluster of fortresses, approachable only from the north. Had its provisions not been destroyed, it is hard to see why it might not have withstood the Romans indefinitely.

As it was, the siege, though conducted with great skill and vigour, lasted from the middle of April till September — five months of constant and desperate fighting. Twelve days were required to break through the hastily built outer wall, and it was not until July that Antonia was taken, and then only after the city had been completely surrounded by a wall. Then the miseries of the besieged city, filled to overflowing with the pilgrims to the Passover, grew indescribable. Without the city captives were crucified by the hundred, and deserters were cut open for the gold they had swallowed. Within the walls famine and civil war filled the streets and houses with unburied dead. Prophets foretold the fearful punishments of God. Portents and wonders in the heaven showed approaching doom. Yet through it all the daily morning and evening sacrifices were kept up until priests and animals alike failed, and on the 17th of July they ceased forever. After this, the siege progressed steadily. Antonia was taken and raised. The beautiful colonnades of the temple were burnt. The outer wall of the temple was broken through, and at last on the tenth day of the month Ab (August) the Romans burst through the burning gates into the sacred area. Titus had hoped to save the temple itself, but some soldier threw a blazing brand into one of its rooms, and the building was soon destroyed. After a fearful slaughter of the inhabitants of the city, Titus began the siege of the upper city in which Simon ben-Giora and John of Gischala made their last desperate stand. The lower city was burned to give room for towers and battering-rams, and after a month the entire city fell into the hands of the Romans (September, 70 A.D.). Thousands of the inhabitants were killed, sold into slavery, or kept for gladiatorial games. John of Gischala was condemned to imprisonment for life. Simon ben-Giora was kept for the triumph at Rome, where he was put to death. The city itself was destroyed as far as any city can be destroyed, and its ruins left in charge of the tenth legion and some auxiliary troops. Although two years were to elapse before the wholesale suicide of the garrison of Sicarii at Masada proclaimed the land at peace, Titus celebrated his victory at Caesarea Philippi, Berytus (Beirut), and Antioch, and in the summer of 71 A.D. was given a triumph in Rome. The noble arch which the senate later erected to his memory still shows in its bas-relief the table of shewbread, the priestly trumpets, and the seven-branched candlestick that, with the rest of the wreckage of the Jewish state, were carried in the great procession.

For the Jewish state had indeed fallen. Vespasian kept Palestine as his private property, a colony of eight hundred veterans was settled at Emmaus just out from Jerusalem, and the Jewish people were everywhere made to pay to the temple of Jupiter Capitolinus the two drachmas they had formerly paid to the support of the temple at Jerusalem. The misery foreseen by Jesus had come — fully, irretrievably. The fall of Jerusalem was the outcome of the Jews' choice as to the kingdom of God. Had they but known the things that pertained to peace!

Yet Judaism was not destroyed, nor the Jewish Messianic hope. The one was to develop in Babylon and Galilee into something severer and farther reaching than Shammai himself could have foreseen, and the other was to blaze forth, not only as a scholar's hope, but as the incentive to new religious war against Hadrian, under Akiba and his Messiah, Bar Cochbar, the Son of the Star. In comparison with these later developments, the Judaism of New Testament times, elaborate as it was, seems almost embryonic. With no country, or temple, or high priest, the only future for Judaism was the Talmud and apologetic Messianism, and each alike bears witness to the earnestness of generations of rabbis.

Yet in neither of these two particulars was to be the greatest significance of the Jew, but rather in that other Messianic movement despised by the rabbis, the Christian church.

For while Pharisee and Zealot, constrained by their scholastic ideals of righteousness, looked for a divinely founded kingdom of the Jews that should be inaugurated by the expulsion of the Romans; and while, maddened by the apparent delay of Jehovah, charlatans and Sicarii and Zealots were turning against the petty oppressions of unworthy governors and plunging the nation into war that the coming of God's kingdom might thus be hastened; the little group of humble men and women who had accepted Jesus as Christ and were finding in his teachings a discipline, had crossed to Greece and Macedonia, and at last had its representatives among the inhabitants of Rome itself. Under the inspiration of Paul it had withstood all efforts to bring the new fraternities under Judaism as a system, and had at last become so strong that few cities of importance in the empire did not contain bands of simple, religious men and women, who were looking for a return of Jesus the Messiah, but were practising none of the requirements of Judaism.

It is, however, a mistake to think of Christianity as standing wholly as the enemy of Judaism. Far more truly is it indebted to Judaism. Without the life and feelings and conditions born of the history of the three centuries we have sketched, the work of Jesus and of Paul would have been very different, if indeed possible. Neither Jesus nor Paul broke utterly with their marvellous nation. Rather, they were the noblest fruitage of Moses and the prophets, and whenever the Christian church names its Christ, it is unconsciously paying tribute to the deep piety of those later Hebrews, who, through persecution and disappointment, with unswerving devotion to their ideas of divine righteousness, looked forward to a time when God would found his kingdom upon the earth, and bequeathed to later generations a faith and an ideal. But, for him who accepts Jesus as the Christ, the faith of Chasidim and Pharisees, of Zealot and Scribe, is no longer national, their ideal has become the story of a Life, and the Kingdom of God is already working its peaceful conquests over humanity.

A NOTE TO THE READER

WE HOPED YOU LOVED THIS BOOK. IF YOU DID, PLEASE LEAVE A REVIEW ON AMAZON TO LET EVERYONE ELSE KNOW WHAT YOU THOUGHT.

WE WOULD ALSO LIKE TO THANK OUR SPONSORS **WWW.DIGITALHISTORYBOOKS.COM** WHO MADE THE PUBLICATION OF THIS BOOK POSSIBLE.

WWW.DIGITALHISTORYBOOKS.COM PROVIDES A WEEKLY NEWSLETTER OF THE BEST DEALS IN HISTORY AND HISTORICAL FICTION.

SIGN UP TO THEIR NEWLSETTER TO FIND OUT MORE ABOUT THEIR LATEST DEALS.

Made in the USA
Middletown, DE
26 May 2020